This selection of George Orwell's writings, from both his novels and non-fiction, gathers together his thoughts on the subject of freedom. It ranges from pieces on individual liberty, society and technology, to political liberty, revolution and the importance of free speech. Orwell's ambition to create a fairer and more egalitarian society is essential inspiration as we strive for freedom and equality in today's world.

ORWELL ON FREEDOM

ORWELL

ON

~~FREEDOM~~

GEORGE ORWELL

Harvill *Secker*

LONDON

1 3 5 7 9 10 8 6 4 2

Harvill Secker, an imprint of Vintage,
20 Vauxhall Bridge Road,
London SW1V 2SA

Harvill Secker is part of the Penguin Random House group of companies
whose addresses can be found at global.penguinrandomhouse.com

Thi ... *Works*
of (... itain

A CIP catalogue record for this book is available from the British Library

ISBN 9781787301405

Typeset in 12/16 pt Bembo MT Pro
by Integra Software Services Pvt. Ltd, Pondicherry

Printed and bound in Great Britain by Clays Ltd, Elcograf S.p.A.

Penguin Random House is committed to a sustainable future for
our business, our readers and our planet. This book is made
from Forest Stewardship Council® certified paper.

Introduction

I first read Orwell as an eighteen-year-old, newly arrived in America for university. It was 1991. In the space of a few years the Soviets had been driven out of Afghanistan, Nelson Mandela had been released from prison, the Berlin Wall had fallen, and democracies were bursting out of totalitarian soil, including in my home nation of Pakistan. I was young enough to believe progress was linear, and that I was entering adulthood just as the world was becoming an irrevocably better place.

Of course I knew even then that the picture was not quite so uncomplicated. Pakistan's three-year-old democracy was floundering; Afghanistan was gripped by civil war and no one much seemed to care just so long as the Soviets weren't involved; and America's war on its former ally, Saddam Hussein, suggested that the lone superpower left standing after the Cold War might be more interested in increasing its economic and political might than in spreading freedom (having grown up during the days of America's close alliance with Pakistan's dictator Muhammad Zia-ul-Haq, I was sceptical about the new world order's commitment to other people's freedoms to begin with). But though I knew all this at an abstract level I was largely undefended against the seductively optimistic mood in America as Bill Clinton, child of the 1960s, came closer to the White House – both he and America sufficiently at ease with themselves for it to be considered a smart political move to appear on MTV and answer the question 'Boxers or briefs?' Oh, the world was good – more than that, it was fun. And *Nineteen Eighty-Four* proved it.

By which I mean, my naive reading of the novel seemed further evidence of the sunniness of the world. I read *Nineteen Eighty-Four* as though it were a piece of fiction that showed us what the world could have been if the Cold

War had turned out differently. But in the world we actually lived in, the world in which I was reading *Nineteen Eighty-Four*, the novel served primarily to underscore the triumph of Democracy with a very capital – or do I mean, capitalist – D. Big Brother and the Thought Police and Newspeak had been defeated. Winston was free.

This is not to say I was dismissive of *Nineteen Eighty-Four*. Quite the contrary. In those student days when it was necessary to decorate the walls and door of your dorm room with evidence of the things by which you wished to be known, I printed out a section of *Nineteen Eighty-Four* and pasted it to my door:

> Winston was dreaming ... The girl with dark hair was coming towards them across the field. With what seemed a single movement she tore off her clothes and flung them disdainfully aside. Her body was white and smooth, but it aroused no desire in him, indeed he barely looked at it. What overwhelmed him in that instant was admiration

for the gesture with which she had thrown her clothes aside. With its grace and carelessness it seemed to annihilate a whole culture, a whole system of thought, as though Big Brother and the Party and the Thought Police could all be swept into nothingness by a single splendid movement of the arm. That too was a gesture belonging to the ancient time. Winston woke up with the word 'Shakespeare' on his lips.

Why did I stick that on my door? Because it said something nice about Shakespeare. That, in 1991, was the most striking part of *Nineteen Eighty-Four* to me. I wonder now if I might have read the novel differently, paid better attention to its warnings, if I had read the letter Orwell wrote to Amy Charlesworth in 1937:

What we call democracy in a capitalist country only remains in being while things are going well; in time of difficulty it turns immediately into Fascism.

It's chilling to read that today as we watch the rise of the far-right across the world, with increasing numbers of voters turning towards the ultra-nationalist Strong Man whose opponents are branded traitors. At the same time, surveillance technology means Big Brother is always watching us, and what's more it turns out that the world of the Internet, which was in its delightful infancy in my undergraduate days, is a new incarnation of the Thought Police – at work improving its algorithms to allow it to enter our minds so it can first know, and then influence, the choices we think we're making of our own free will. All this before we even get started on all those terms of Newspeak that are part of twenty-first-century English, from 'collateral damage' to 'rendition' to 'fake news'. In these times, no work of fiction or non-fiction seems more prescient or apt than *Nineteen Eighty-Four*. Any writer at work today, seeking a way to respond to the terrifying new world, could do worse than ask the question: 'What would Orwell write?'

★

Because Orwell was Orwell, committed to independence of thought and writing uncomfortable truths, I wish to claim that it is in his spirit and in his honour that I'm able to say in this introduction – usually a place of praise – that I do not always find him agreeable. Far from it. I had to put down this collection of work and walk away from it for a considerable space of time after I read the following sentences, from 'Will Freedom Die with Capitalism?' (1941):

The enemies of Western civilisation are fond of pointing out that the comparative peacefulness and decency of life in the democracies are simply the reflection of a high national income, which for a hundred years past has been based largely on coloured labour. This is true, but it is rather like saying 'This field is only more fertile than that because it was manured last year.' Our scruples are not less real because we have bought them with the blood of Indian coolies. A hatred of civil violence and a respect for freedom of speech are definite factors in Western life.

This, coming from an anti-imperialist, is in its own way worse than claims by the supporters of empire that the enterprise was a civilising mission from which the natives greatly benefited. Worse, because it disappoints. Orwell *was* anti-imperialist – he recognised that for the colonised the experience of empire was one of degradation, and that the colonisers themselves are warped by their experiences while in the colonies. But there are places in which his anti-imperialism has to square off against his patriotism, and anti-imperialism ends up limping away, bloodied and defeated. At one time he marvels at how peaceful the British Empire is, at another he pauses in his anti-imperial analysis to comment how much better that British Empire is to the empires that will supplant it. It's hard now to imagine how a writer of his acumen could write that Englishmen spill the blood of Indian coolies but hate civil violence, as though a nation can have one character abroad and another one at home. Had he lived longer, might he have thought about this differently? His England was such a homogeneous place – with class the only way of differentiating people; it is hard not to wonder how he would have reacted to the formerly colonised people moving to Britain, bringing all that violent history 'home'. I like to think he would have acknowledged the partiality of his own vision.

But perhaps he wouldn't have, and this turns out to be a useful matter to consider. As I said, I don't always find Orwell agreeable (empire aside, there's also his less than stellar record with regard to writing about women), but that's never reason not to read him, or not to praise his contributions to the novel, and to intellectual life. He serves as a reminder, in this age of anger and offence, that the presence of a contradiction or a limitation is hardly reason to dismiss or denounce a writer's work. Equally, he serves as a reminder that a pedestal is no place for a writer. 'Was he always right, or good?' is no kind of question to ask of a writer. Ask instead, 'Does the work still retain value when you subject it to the harshest critical fire?' In Orwell's case, that question can't ever be seen as other than rhetorical.

★

> Perhaps it will be frankest to approach it first of all from the personal angle. I am a writer. The impulse of every writer is to 'keep out of politics'. What he wants is to be left alone so that he can go on writing books in peace.

So Orwell wrote in 1938. Arguably the greatest political writer in the English language insisting that every writer wants to keep out of politics. It was, of course, a precursor to saying that the world will not allow a writer to do such a thing. But if I am to follow Orwell and be frank in approaching things from the personal angle, I might as well confess right now that what I most admire in Orwell, the aspect of his work to which I wish more people would pay attention right now, is his use of the novel as a form for political writing. Even though

Nineteen Eighty-Four is regularly – and rightly – listed as one of the greatest novels of the last century (or ever), we continue to live in an England in which too many writers – most of whom you'd expect to know better – shy away from the term 'political novel'. Oh no, no, no, they say, when confronted with that label about their work. Those of us who don't shy away from it quickly become accustomed to being asked in tentative terms: 'How do you feel about the term "political novel"?', as though the interlocutor knows an insult is being smuggled in with that term, and wonders if you realise it too. Somewhere we developed the ridiculous notion that political means polemical when used to describe a novel (this can probably be traced back to the Cold War in which a dichotomy was set up between the Political Novels of the Soviets and the Freedom to be Individual novels of Americans). A consequence of this depoliticising of the novel is that today's Orwells are far more likely to be writing non-fiction than fiction. I've heard several writers of my acquaintance, whose sentences and politics I deeply admire, express the view that the world feels too urgent for novels. It's true, of course, that novels take more time to write and publish than newspaper or magazine articles – but what Orwell knew was that there is something in a novel that makes up for its lack of immediacy, and that is the imagination. There is a power in saying *this is* and *this might be* but a whole other power to marrying analysis with imagination, and plunging your readers deep into lives that are not their own (but might be, and at their best almost feel as if they are). It is no disrespect to all Orwell's non-fiction writings to say *Nineteen Eighty-Four* alone outweighs them in its ability to make us think and feel and see the world around us differently – and in its ability to renew itself for the new (but old) worlds in which we are living.

This takes me back to my eighteen-year-old self, the one who read *Nineteen Eighty-Four* and decided the passage in it most worthy of homage was one about Shakespeare. If Shakespeare can be seen to stand in for imagination and creativity expressed in language, then perhaps that eighteen-year-old didn't get it so wrong after all. In an age of anger and offence the indirection and empathy of the novel, its multiplicity of voices, its belief that we can understand the most profound differences, its seductive qualities of plot and character, are gifts we'd be foolish to try to keep separate from the most urgent conversations of our time. We are living in an Orwellian world – what we need in response are Orwellian novels.

Kamila Shamsie
September 2018

'First, what is a tramp?'

from 'A Day in the Life of a Tramp'
Le Progrès Civique, 5 January 1929
Translated into English by
Janet Percival and Ian Willison

First, what is a tramp?

A tramp is a native English species. These are his distinguishing characteristics: he has no money, he is dressed in rags, he walks about twenty kilometres a day and never sleeps two nights together in the same place.

In short, he is a wanderer, living on charity, roaming around on foot day after day for years, crossing England from end to end many times in his wanderings.

He has no job, home or family, no possessions in the world apart from the rags covering his poor body; he lives at the expense of the community.

No-one knows how many individuals make up the tramp population. Thirty thousand?

Fifty thousand? Perhaps a hundred thousand in England and Wales when unemployment is particularly bad.

The tramp does not wander for his own amusement, or because he has inherited the nomadic instincts of his ancestors; he is trying first and foremost to avoid starving to death.

It is not difficult to see why; the tramp is unemployed as a result of the state of the English economy. So, to exist, he must have recourse to public or private charity. To assist him, the authorities have created *asiles* (workhouses) where the destitute can find food and shelter.

These places are about twenty kilometres apart, and no-one can stay in any one spike more than once a month. Hence the endless pilgrimages of tramps who, if they want to eat and sleep with a roof over their heads, must seek a new resting-place every night.

That is the explanation for the existence of tramps. Now let us see what sort of life they lead. It will be sufficient to look at just one day,

for the days are all the same for these unfortunate inhabitants of one of the richest countries
in the world. [...]

★

Let us take one of them as he comes out of the
spike at about ten in the morning.

He is about twenty kilometres from the next
workhouse. He will probably take five hours to
walk that distance, and will arrive at his desti-
nation at about three in the afternoon.

He will not rest much on the way, because
the police, who look on tramps with a suspi-
cious eye, will make quick work of sending
him packing from any town or village where
he might try to stop. [...] But the spike does not
open until six in the evening. Three weary
hours to kill in the company of the other tramps
who are already waiting. The herd of human
beings, haggard, unshaven, filthy and tattered,
grows from minute to minute. Soon there are
a hundred unemployed men representing nearly
every trade.

Miners and cotton-spinners, victims of the unemployment which is raging in the North of England, form the majority but all trades are represented, skilled or not.

Their age? From sixteen to seventy.

Their sex? There are around two women for every fifty tramps.

Here and there, an imbecile jabbers meaningless words. Some men are so weak and decrepit that one wonders how they could possibly walk twenty kilometres.

Their clothes strike you as grotesque, tattered and revoltingly filthy.

Their faces make you think of the face of some wild animal, not perhaps a dangerous one, but one which has become at once savage and timorous through lack of rest and care.

★

[...] They have come from all four corners of England and Wales, and tell each other their adventures, discussing without much hope the likelihood of finding work on the way.

Many have met before in some spike at the other end of the country for their tracks cross again and again in their ceaseless wanderings.

These workhouses are miserable and sordid caravanserais where the miserable English pilgrims assemble for a few hours before scattering again in all directions. [...]

When a tramp does come by some money, which he has worked for or begged on the way, his first thought is to buy tobacco, but mostly he has to make do with cigarette-ends picked up from the pavement or road. The spike only gives him his board: for the rest, clothes, tobacco etc. he has to shift for himself.

*

But it is nearly time for the gates of the spike to open. The tramps have got up, and are queuing by the wall of the huge building, a vile yellow cube of brick, built in some distant suburb, and which might be mistaken for a prison.

A few more minutes and the heavy gates swing open and the herd of human beings enters.

The resemblance between one of these spikes and a prison is even more striking once you are through the gates. In the middle of an empty yard, surrounded by high brick walls stands the main building containing bare-walled cells, a bathroom, the administrative offices, and a tiny room furnished with plain deal benches which serves as a dining-room. Everything is as ugly and as sinister as you care to imagine.

The prison atmosphere can be found everywhere. Uniformed officials bully the tramps and push them about, never neglecting to remind them that in coming into the workhouse they have given up all their rights and all their freedom.

The tramp's name and trade are written in a register. Then he is made to have a bath, and his clothes and personal possessions are taken away. Then he is given a coarse cotton workhouse shirt for the night.

If he should happen to have any money, it is confiscated, but if he admits to more than two francs [fourpence] he will not be allowed into the spike and will have to find a bed somewhere else.

As a result those tramps – there are not many of them – who have more than two francs have taken pains to hide their money in the toes of their boots, making sure they are not observed, for this fraud could be punished with imprisonment.

After his bath, the tramp, whose clothes have now been taken away, receives his supper: half a pound of bread with a little margarine and a half-litre of tea.

The bread made specially for tramps is terrible. It is grey, always stale, and has a disagreeable taste which makes one think that the flour it is made from comes from tainted grain.

Even the tea is as bad as it can be, but the tramps drink it gladly, as it warms and comforts them after the exhaustion of the day.

This unappetising meal is gulped down in five minutes. After that, the tramps are ordered into the cells where they will spend the night.

These cells, real prison cells of brick or stone, are about twelve feet by six. There is no artificial light – the only source of light is a narrow barred window very high up in the wall and a spyhole in the door which allows the guards to keep an eye on the inmates.

Sometimes the cell contains a bed, but normally the tramps have to sleep on the floor with only three blankets for bedding.

There are often no pillows, and for this reason the unfortunate inmates are allowed to keep their coats to roll into a sort of cushion for their heads.

Usually the room is terribly cold, and as a result of long use the blankets have become so thin that they offer no protection at all against the severity of the cold.

As soon as the tramps have entered their cells, the doors are firmly bolted on the outside: they will not open until seven o'clock next morning.

Usually there are two inmates in each cell. Walled up in their little prison for twelve weary hours with nothing to keep out the cold but a cotton shirt and three thin blankets, the poor wretches suffer cruelly from the cold and the lack of the most elementary comfort.

The places are nearly always bug-infested, and the tramp, a prey to vermin, his limbs worn out, spends hours and hours tossing and turning in a vain wait for sleep.

If he does manage to fall asleep for a few minutes, the discomfort of sleeping on a hard floor soon wakes him up again.

The wily old tramps who have been living like this for fifteen or twenty years, and have become philosophical as a result, spend their nights talking. They will rest for an hour or two next day in a field, under some hedge which they find more welcoming than the spike. But the younger ones, not yet hardened by familiarity with the routine, struggle and groan in the darkness, waiting impatiently for the morning to bring their release.

And yet, when the sunlight finally shines into their prison, they consider with gloom and desperation the prospect of another day exactly like the one before.

Finally, the cells are unlocked. It is time for the doctor's visit – indeed, the tramps will not be released until this formality is completed.

The doctor is usually late, and the tramps have to wait for his inspection, lined up half-naked in a passage. Then one can get an idea of their physical condition.

What bodies and what faces!

Many of them have congenital malforma-tions. Several suffer from hernias, and wear trusses. Almost everyone has deformed feet covered in sores as a result of lengthy tramping in ill-fitting boots. The old men are nothing but skin and bone. All have sagging muscles, and the wretched look of men who do not get a square meal from one end of the year to the other.

Their emaciated features, premature wrin-kles, unshaven beards, everything about them tells of insufficient food and lack of sleep.

But here comes the doctor. His inspection is as rapid as it is cursory. It is designed, after all, merely to detect whether any of the tramps are showing the symptoms of smallpox.

The doctor glances at each of the tramps in turn rapidly up and down, front and back.

Now most of them are suffering from some disease or other. Some of them, almost complete imbeciles, are hardly capable of taking care of themselves. Nevertheless they will be released as long as they are free from the dreaded marks of smallpox.

The authorities do not care whether they are in good or bad health, as long as they are not suffering from an infectious disease.

After the doctor's inspection, the tramps get dressed again. Then, in the cold light of day, you can really get a good look at the clothes the poor devils wear to protect themselves against the ravages of the English climate.

These disparate articles of clothing – mostly begged from door to door – are hardly fit for the dustbin. Grotesque, ill-fitting [...] They have been repaired as far as possible, with all kinds of patches. String does duty for missing buttons. Underclothes are nothing but filthy tatters, holes held together by dirt.

Some of them have no underclothes. Many do not even have socks; after binding their toes in rags, they slide their bare feet into boots whose leather, hardened by sun and rain, has lost all suppleness.

It is a fearful sight watching tramps getting ready.

Once they are dressed, the tramps receive their breakfast, identical to the previous night's supper.

Then they are lined up like soldiers in the yard of the spike, where the guards set them to work.

Some will wash the floor, others will chop wood, break coal, do a variety of jobs until ten o'clock, when the signal to leave is given.

They are given back any personal property confiscated the previous evening. To this is added half a pound of bread and a piece of cheese for their midday meal, or sometimes, but less often, a ticket which can be exchanged at specified cafés along the way for bread and tea to the value of three francs [sixpence].

A little after ten o'clock, the gates of the spike swing open to let loose a crowd of wretched and filthy destitute men who scatter over the countryside.

Each one is making for a fresh spike where he will be treated in exactly the same way.

And for months, years, decades perhaps the tramp will know no other existence.

*

In conclusion, we should note that the food for each tramp consists, all in all, of around 750 grammes [2 pounds] of bread with a little margarine and cheese, and a pint of tea a day; this is clearly an insufficient diet for a man who must cover twenty kilometres a day on foot.

To supplement his diet, to obtain clothing, tobacco and the thousand other things he might need, the tramp must beg when he cannot find work (and he hardly ever finds work) – beg or steal.

Now begging is against the law in England, and many a tramp has become acquainted with His Majesty's prisons because of it.

It is a vicious circle; if he does not beg, he dies of starvation; if he begs, he is breaking the law.

The life of these tramps is degrading and demoralising. In a very short time it can make an active man unemployable and a sponger.

Moreover it is desperately monotonous. The only pleasure for tramps is coming by a few shillings unexpectedly; this gives them the chance to eat their fill for once or to go on a drinking spree. [...]

Finally the tramp, who has not committed any crime, and who is, when all is said and done, simply a victim of unemployment, is condemned to live more wretchedly than the worst criminal. He is a slave with a semblance of liberty which is worse than the most cruel slavery.

He is a slave with
a semblance of liberty
which is worse than the
most cruel slavery.

When we reflect upon his miserable destiny, which is shared by thousands of men in England, the obvious conclusion is that society would be treating him more kindly by shutting him up for the remainder of his days in prison, where he would at least enjoy relative comfort.

'The stars are a free show; it don't cost anything to use your eyes.'

From *Down and Out in Paris and London* (1933)

The next morning we began looking once more for Paddy's friend, who was called Bozo, and was a screever – that is, a pavement artist. Addresses did not exist in Paddy's world, but he had a vague idea that Bozo might be found in Lambeth, and in the end we ran across him on the Embankment, where he had established himself not far from Waterloo Bridge. He was kneeling on the pavement with a box of chalks, copying a sketch of Winston Churchill from a penny note-book. The likeness was not at all bad. Bozo was a small, dark, hook-nosed man, with curly hair growing low on his head. His right leg was dreadfully deformed, the foot being twisted heel forward in a way horrible to see. From his appearance one could have taken

17

him for a Jew, but he used to deny this vigorously. He spoke of his hook-nose as 'Roman', and was proud of his resemblance to some Roman Emperor – it was Vespasian, I think.

Bozo had a strange way of talking, Cockneyfied and yet very lucid and expressive. It was as though he had read good books but had never troubled to correct his grammar. For a while Paddy and I stayed on the Embankment, talking, and Bozo gave us an account of the screeving trade. I repeat what he said more or less in his own words:

'I'm what they call a serious screever. I don't draw in blackboard chalks like these others, I use proper colours the same as what painters use; bloody expensive they are, especially the reds. I use five bobs' worth of colours in a long day, and never less than two bobs' worth. Cartoons is my line – you know, politics and cricket and that. Look here' – he showed me his note-book – 'here's likenesses of all the political blokes, what I've copied from the papers. I have a different cartoon every day. For instance, when the Budget was on I had one of Winston trying to push an elephant marked "Debt", and underneath I wrote, "Will he budge it?" See? You can have cartoons about any of the parties, but you mustn't put anything in favour of Socialism, because the police won't stand it. Once I did a cartoon of a boa constrictor marked Capital swallowing a rabbit marked Labour. The copper came along and saw it, and he says, "You rub that out, and look sharp about it," he says. I had to rub it out. The copper's got the right to move you on for loitering, and it's no good giving them a back answer.'

[...] Bozo seemed an interesting man, and I was anxious to see more of him. That evening I went down to the Embankment to meet him, as he had arranged to take Paddy and myself to a lodging-house south of the river. Bozo washed his pictures off the pavement and counted his takings – it was about sixteen shillings, of which he said twelve or thirteen would be profit. We walked down into Lambeth. Bozo limped slowly, with a queer crab-like gait, half sideways, dragging his smashed foot behind him. He carried a stick in each hand

19

and slung his box of colours over his shoulder. As we were crossing the bridge he stopped in one of the alcoves to rest. He fell silent for a minute or two, and to my surprise I saw that he was looking at the stars. He touched my arm and pointed to the sky with his stick.

'Say, will you look at Aldebaran! Look at the colour. Like a – great blood orange!'

From the way he spoke he might have been an art critic in a picture gallery. I was astonished. I confessed that I did not know which Aldebaran was – indeed, I had never even noticed that the stars were of different colours. Bozo began to give me some elementary hints on astronomy, pointing out the chief constellations. He seemed concerned at my ignorance. I said to him, surprised:

'You seem to know a lot about stars.'

'Not a great lot. I know a bit, though. I got two letters from the Astronomer Royal thanking me for writing about meteors. Now and again I go out at night and watch for meteors. The stars are a free show; it don't cost anything to use your eyes.'

'What a good idea! I should never have thought of it.'

'Well, you got to take an interest in something. It don't follow that because a man's on the road he can't think of anything but tea-and-two-slices.'

'But isn't it very hard to take an interest in things – things like stars – living this life?'

'Screeving, you mean? Not necessarily. It don't need turn you into a bloody rabbit – that is, not if you set your mind to it.'

'It seems to have that effect on most people.'

'Of course. Look at Paddy – a tea-swilling old moocher, only fit to scrounge for fag-ends. That's the way most of them go. I despise them. But you don't need get like that. If you've got any education, it don't matter to you if you're on the road for the rest of your life.'

'Well, I've found just the contrary,' I said. 'It seems to me that when you take a man's money away he's fit for nothing from that moment.'

'No, not necessarily. If you set yourself to it, you can live the same life, rich or poor. You can still keep on with your books and your ideas. You just got to say to yourself, "I'm a free man in here"' – he tapped his forehead – 'and you're all right.'

'You just got to say to yourself,
"I'm a free man in here"'
– he tapped his forehead –
'and you're all right.'

'You are the hopeless slave of money until you have enough of it to live on'

from *Keep the Aspidistra Flying* (1936)

They thought Gordon must have gone mad. Over and over again he tried, quite vainly, to explain to them why he would not yield himself to the servitude of a 'good' job. 'But what are you going to live on? What are you going to live on?' was what they all wailed at him. He refused to think seriously about it. Of course, he still harboured the notion that he could make a living of sorts by 'writing'. By this time he had got to know Ravelston, editor of Antichrist, and Ravelston, besides printing his poems, managed to get him books to review occasionally. His literary prospects were not so bleak as they had been six years ago. But still, it was not the desire to 'write' that was his real motive. To get out of the money-world—that was what he wanted. Vaguely he looked forward to some kind of moneyless, anchorite existence. He had a feeling that if you genuinely despise money you can keep going somehow, like the birds of the air. He forgot that the birds of the air don't pay room-rent. The poet starving in a garret—but starving, somehow, not uncomfortably—that was his vision of himself.

The next seven months were devastating. They scared him and almost broke his spirit. He learned what it means to live for weeks on end on bread and margarine, to try to 'write' when you are half starved, to pawn your clothes, to sneak trembling up the stairs when you owe three weeks' rent and your landlady is listening for you. Moreover, in those seven months he wrote practically nothing. The first effect of poverty is that it kills thought. He grasped, as though it were a new discovery, that you do not escape from money merely by being moneyless. On the contrary, you are the hopeless slave of money until you have enough of it to live on—a 'competence', as the beastly middle-class phrase goes. Finally he was turned out of his room, after a vulgar row. He was three days and four nights in the street. It was bloody. Three mornings, on the advice of another man he met on the Embankment, he spent in Billingsgate, helping to shove fish-barrows up the twisty little hills from Billingsgate into Eastcheap. 'Twopence an up' was what you got, and the work knocked hell out of your thigh muscles. There were crowds of people on the same job, and you had to wait your turn; you were lucky if you made eight-eenpence between four in the morning and nine. After three days of it Gordon gave up. What was the use? He was beaten. There was nothing for it but to go back to his family, borrow some money and find another job.

'It is quite true that we ought all to combine against Fascism, but then one has got to decide what Fascism is.'

to Amy Charlesworth
30 August 1937, typewritten

The Stores Wallington Nr. Baldock HERTS.

Dear Miss Charlesworth,

Many thanks for your letter, which at present I can't find, but no doubt it will turn up presently, and then I will get your address from it. I enquired where you could get the 'New Leader' in Manchester, and am told that you can get it at any of the following:

Garner, 56 Worthington Street, Old Trafford, Manchester 16.

Lewis, 379 Ashton New Road, Bradford, Manchester.

J. Hodgetts, 57 Lynn Street, West Gorton, Manchester.

I think you will find it worth an occasional
ld. It is a poor little paper, but often has the
truth in it when other papers don't.

As to the P.O.U.M.,⋆ the Communist
Party in Spain etc. It is not exactly true that
the P.O.U.M. was trying to 'set up a soviet' in
opposition to the Government. Where the
P.O.U.M., and you might also say the Anarchists, differed from the Government and the
Communist Party, was in saying that Franco
must be resisted not in the name of democracy as it exists in England, France etc., but in
the name of workers' government. This is not
so theoretical as it sounds, because it meant an
actual difference of policy. When the revolution broke out the workers did in many
parts of Spain establish the beginnings of a

⋆ Publisher's note: the Partido Obrero de Unificación Marx-
ista (the Workers' Party of Marxist Unification), in whose
militia Orwell fought in the Spanish Civil War. Communist
Party propaganda accusing POUM of espionage and
collaborating with the Fascists, combined with attacks on
people with POUM connections (which were widely
circulated in Britain), affected Orwell deeply.

workers' government, seizing land and factories, setting up local committees, etc., etc. The Government, which is largely under control of the Communist Party, has managed to undo most of this, at first by appealing to the workers not to endanger the war, later, when they felt themselves stronger, by force. I think the P.O.U.M. and the others were quite right to resist this process and would perhaps have been right to resist it even by open rebellion, though they never did so. It is quite true that we ought all to combine against Fascism, but then one has got to decide what Fascism is. If Fascism means suppression of political liberty and free speech, imprisonment without trial etc., then the present regime in Spain *is* Fascism; so in apparently fighting against Fascism you come straight back to Fascism. I don't mean that the rule of the present Government is no better than what Franco would set up if he won, but it is only different in degree, not in kind. What emerges from this – or so it appears to me – is that Fascism has no real opposite except Socialism. You can't fight against Fascism in the name of 'democracy,' because what we call democracy in a capitalist country only remains in being while things are going well; in time of difficulty it turns immediately into Fascism. The only thing that can prevent this is for the workers to keep the power in their own hands. Obviously one can't have complete workers' control and Socialism all in a moment, but the workers ought to cling onto every scrap of power they possess, whether, as in England, it is in the form of democratic institutions, or, as in Spain at the beginning of the war, in the fact that the workers have arms in their hands and have seized some of the means of production. If they listen to anyone who says to them, 'You must give up this, that and the other for the common good,' they will be cheated every time. This is what happened in Spain. The Communist Party propagandists said that the workers had no need to keep direct control on factories, transport etc., because they were adequately represented in the Government, which contained ministers representing the trade unions. Later, of course, when the arms had for the most part been got out of the workers' hands and the Communist–Liberal clique was in a stronger position, the trade-union representatives were turned out of the Government and you now have a Government which does not contain one minister representing any working-class party. The only thing that could excuse this is military necessity, and of course this excuse has been used all along. But as a matter of fact the present Government (the Negrin Government, dating from May) has been much less successful in a military sense than the previous ones. It has worked itself into a position of absolute power and put most of its opponents in jail, but it is not winning the war. I doubt indeed whether the war can now be won unless France intervenes. To win a war you have either got to have a preponderance of arms, which the Government has not got and is not likely to have, or you have got to arouse enthusiasm among the people. But no one can get up much enthusiasm for a

Government which puts you in jail if you open your mouth.

Excuse me always lecturing you about this. But what I saw in Spain has upset me so much that I talk about it to everybody. And the English papers have told such frightful lies about the whole business, the left-wing papers (*News Chronicle* and *Daily Worker*) almost worse than the right-wing ones. It is desperately necessary to get people to see through the humbug that is talked about 'fighting against Fascism,' or the next thing we know we shall find ourselves fighting another imperialist war (against Germany) which will be dressed up as a war 'against Fascism,' and then another ten million men will be dead before people grasp that Fascism and so-called democracy are Tweedledum and Tweedledee.

I think you asked about my voice.★ It is much better, in fact I can shout to quite a

---

★ Publisher's note: three months before this letter was written, Orwell had been shot in the throat by a sniper on the front line in Spain.

No one can get up much enthusiasm for a Government which puts you in jail if you open your mouth distance now, but I still can't modulate it enough to sing, so I suppose one vocal cord is permanently paralysed.

Yours sincerely
Eric Blair

'The freedom of the Press in Britain was always something of a fake, because in the last resort, money controls opinion'

'Why I Join the I.L.P.'
The *New Leader*, 24 June 1938

Perhaps it will be frankest to approach it first of all from the personal angle.

I am a writer. The impulse of every writer is to 'keep out of politics.' What he wants is to be left alone so that he can go on writing books in peace. But unfortunately it is becoming obvious that this ideal is no more practicable than that of the petty shopkeeper who hopes to preserve his independence in the teeth of the chain-stores.

To begin with, the era of free speech is closing down. The freedom of the Press in Britain was always something of a fake, because in the last resort, money controls opinion; still, so long as the legal right to say what you like exists, there are always loopholes for an unorthodox writer. For some years past I have managed to make the Capitalist class pay me several pounds a week for writing books against Capitalism. But I do not delude myself that this state of affairs is going to last for ever. We have seen what has happened to the freedom of the Press in Italy and Germany, and it will happen here sooner or later. The time is coming – not next year, perhaps not for ten or twenty years, but it is coming – when every writer will have the choice of being silenced altogether or of producing the dope that a privileged minority demands.

I have got to struggle against that, just as I have got to struggle against castor oil, rubber truncheons and concentration-camps. And the only regime which, in the long run, will dare to permit freedom of speech is a Socialist regime. If Fascism triumphs I am finished as a writer – that is to say, finished in my only effective capacity. That of itself would be a sufficient reason for joining a Socialist party.

I have put the personal aspect first, but obviously it is not the only one.

It is not possible for any thinking person to live in such a society as our own without wanting to change it. For perhaps ten years past I have had some grasp of the real nature of Capitalist society. I have seen British Imperialism at work in Burma, and I have seen something of the effects of poverty and unemployment in Britain. In so far as I have struggled against the system, it has been mainly by writing books which I hoped would influence the reading public. I shall continue to do that, of course, but at a moment like the present writing books is not enough. The tempo of events is quickening; the dangers which once seemed a generation distant are staring us in the face. One has got to be actively a Socialist, not merely sympathetic to Socialism, or one plays into the hands of our always-active enemies.

Why the I.L.P. more than another?

Because the I.L.P. is the only British party – at any rate the only one large enough to be worth considering – which aims at anything I should regard as Socialism.

I do not mean that I have lost all faith in the Labour Party. My most earnest hope is that the Labour Party will win a clear majority in the next General Election. But we know what the history of the Labour Party has been, and we know the terrible temptation of the present moment – the temptation to fling every principle overboard in order to prepare for an Imperialist war. It is vitally necessary that there should be in existence some body of people who can be depended on, even in the face of persecution, not to compromise their Socialist principles.

I believe that the I.L.P. is the only party which, as a party, is likely to take the right line either against Imperialist war or against Fascism when this appears in its British form. And meanwhile the I.L.P. is not backed by any monied interest, and is systematically libelled from several quarters. Obviously it needs all the help it can get, including any help I can give it myself.

Finally, I was with the I.L.P. contingent in Spain. I never pretended, then or since, to agree in every detail with the policy the P.O.U.M.

put forward and the I.L.P. supported, but the general course of events has borne it out. The things I saw in Spain brought home to me the fatal danger of mere negative 'anti-Fascism.' Once I had grasped the essentials of the situation in Spain I realised that the I.L.P. was the only British party I felt like joining – and also the only party I could join with at least the certainty that I would never be led up the garden path in the name of Capitalist democracy.

'When a white man turns tyrant it is his own freedom that he destroys.'

from 'Shooting an Elephant'
New Writing 2, Autumn 1936

In Moulmein, in Lower Burma, I was hated by large numbers of people – the only time in my life that I have been important enough for this to happen to me. I was subdivisional police officer of the town, and in an aimless, petty kind of way anti-European feeling was very bitter. No one had the guts to raise a riot, but if a European woman went through the bazaars alone somebody would probably spit betel juice over her dress. As a police officer I was an obvious target and was baited whenever it seemed safe to do so. When a nimble Burman tripped me up on the football field and the referee (another Burman) looked the other way, the crowd yelled with hideous laughter. This happened more than once. In the end the sneering yellow faces of young men that met me everywhere, the insults hooted after me when I was at a safe distance, got badly on my nerves. The young Buddhist priests were the worst of all. There were several thousands of them in the town and none of them seemed to have anything to do except stand on street corners and jeer at Europeans.

All this was perplexing and upsetting. For at that time I had already made up my mind that imperialism was an evil thing and the sooner I chucked up my job and got out of it the better. Theoretically – and secretly, of course – I was all for the Burmese and all against their oppressors, the British. As for the job I was doing, I hated it more bitterly than I can perhaps make clear. In a job like that you see the dirty work of Empire at close quarters. The wretched prisoners huddling in the stinking cages of the lock-ups, the grey, cowed faces of the long-term convicts, the scarred buttocks of the men who had been flogged with bamboos – all these oppressed me with an intolerable sense of guilt. But I could get nothing into perspective. I was young and ill-educated and I had had to think out my problems in the utter silence that is imposed on every Englishman in the East. I did not even know that the British Empire is dying, still less did I know that it is a great deal better than the younger empires that are going to supplant it. All I knew was that I was stuck between my hatred of the empire I served and my rage against the evil-spirited little beasts who tried to make my job impossible. With one part of my mind I thought of the British Raj as an unbreakable tyranny, as something clamped down, in saecula saeculorum, upon the will of prostrate peoples; with another part I thought that the greatest joy in the world would be to drive a bayonet into a Buddhist priest's guts. Feelings like these are the normal by-products of imperialism; ask any Anglo-Indian official, if you can catch him off duty.

One day something happened which in a roundabout way was enlightening. It was a tiny incident in itself, but it gave me a better glimpse than I had had before of the real nature of imperialism – the real motives for which despotic governments act. Early one morning the sub-inspector at a police station the other end of the town rang me up on the phone and said that an elephant was ravaging the bazaar. Would I please come and do something about it? I did not know what I could do, but I wanted to see what was happening and I got on to a pony and started out.

[. . .] It was a very poor quarter, a labyrinth of squalid bamboo huts, thatched with palm-leaf, winding all over a steep hillside. I remember that it was a cloudy stuffy morning at the beginning of the rains. We began questioning the people as to where the elephant had gone, and, as usual, failed to get any definite information. That is invariably the case in the East; a story always sounds clear enough at a distance, but the nearer you get to the scene of events the vaguer it becomes. [. . .] I rounded the hut and saw a man's dead body sprawling in the mud. He was an Indian, a black Dravidian coolie, almost naked, and he could not have been dead many minutes. The people said that the elephant had come suddenly upon him round the corner of the hut, caught him with its trunk, put its foot on his back and ground him into the earth. This was the rainy season and the ground was soft, and his face had scored a trench a foot deep and a couple of yards long. He was lying on his belly with arms crucified and head sharply twisted to one side. His face was coated with mud, the eyes wide open, the teeth bared and grinning with an expression of unendurable agony. (Never tell me, by the way, that the dead look peaceful. Most of the corpses I have seen looked devilish.) The friction of the great beast's foot had stripped the skin from his back as neatly as one skins a rabbit. As soon as I saw the dead man I sent an orderly to a friend's house nearby to borrow an elephant rifle.

[. . .] As I started forward practically the whole population of the quarter flocked out of the houses and followed me. They had seen the rifle and were all shouting excitedly that I was going to shoot the elephant. They had not shown much interest in the elephant when he was merely ravaging their homes, but it was different now that he was going to be shot. It was a bit of fun to them, as it would be to an

English crowd; besides, they wanted the meat. It made me vaguely uneasy. I had no intention of shooting the elephant – I had merely sent for the rifle to defend myself if necessary – and it is always unnerving to have a crowd following you. I marched down the hill, looking and feeling a fool, with the rifle over my shoulder and an ever-growing army of people jostling at my heels. At the bottom, when you got away from the huts, there was a metalled road and beyond that a miry waste of paddy fields a thousand yards across, not yet ploughed but soggy from the first rains and dotted with coarse grass. The elephant was standing eighty yards from the road, his left side towards us. He took not the slightest notice of the crowd's approach. He was tearing up bunches of grass, beating them against his knees to clean them and stuffing them into his mouth.

I had halted on the road. As soon as I saw the elephant I knew with perfect certainty that I ought not to shoot him. It is a serious matter to shoot a working elephant – it is compara- ble to destroying a huge and costly piece of machinery – and obviously one ought not to do it if it can possibly be avoided. And at that distance, peacefully eating, the elephant looked no more dangerous than a cow. I thought then and I think now that his attack of 'must' was already passing off; in which case he would merely wander harmlessly about until the mahout came back and caught him. Moreover, I did not in the least want to shoot him. I decided that I would watch him for a little while to make sure that he did not turn savage again, and then go home.

But at that moment I glanced round at the crowd that had followed me. It was an immense crowd, two thousand at the least and growing every minute. It blocked the road for a long distance on either side. I looked at the sea of yellow faces above the garish clothes – faces all happy and excited over this bit of fun, all certain that the elephant was going to be shot. They were watching me as they would watch a conjuror about to perform a trick. They did not like me, but with the magical rifle in my hands I was momentarily worth watching. And suddenly

I realized that I should have to shoot the elephant after all. The people expected it of me and I had got to do it; I could feel their two thousand wills pressing me forward, irresistibly. And it was at this moment, as I stood there with the rifle in my hands, that I first grasped the hollowness, the futility of the white man's dominion in the East. Here was I, the white man with his gun, standing in front of the unarmed native crowd – seemingly the leading actor of the piece; but in reality I was only an absurd puppet pushed to and fro by the will of those yellow faces behind. I perceived in this moment that when the white man turns tyrant it is his own freedom that he destroys. He becomes a sort of hollow, posing dummy, the conventionalized figure of a sahib. For it is the condition of his rule that he shall spend his life in trying to impress the 'natives,' and so in every crisis he has got to do what the 'natives' expect of him. He wears a mask, and his face grows to fit it. I had got to shoot the elephant. I had committed myself to doing it when I sent for the rifle. A sahib has got to act like a sahib; he has got to appear resolute, to know his own mind and do definite things. To come all that way, rifle in hand, with two thousand people marching at my heels, and then to trail feebly away, having done nothing – no, that was impossible. The crowd would laugh at me. And my whole life, every white man's life in the East, was one long struggle not to be laughed at.

'Why not let the machine do the work and the men go and do something else?'

From *The Road to Wigan Pier* (1937)

The function of the machine is to save work. In a fully mechanised world all the dull drudgery will be done by machinery, leaving us free for more interesting pursuits. So expressed, this sounds splendid. It makes one sick to see half a dozen men sweating their guts out to dig a trench for a water-pipe, when some easily devised machine would scoop the earth out in a couple of minutes. Why not let the machine do the work and the men go and do something else? But presently the question arises, what else are they to do? Supposedly they are set free from 'work' in order that they may do something which is not 'work'. But what is work and what is not work? Is it work to dig, to carpenter, to plant trees, to fell trees, to ride, to fish, to hunt, to feed chickens, to play the piano, to take photographs, to build a house, to cook, to sew, to trim hats, to mend motor-bicycles? All of these things are work to somebody, and all of them are play to somebody. There are in fact very few activities which cannot be classed either as work or play according as you choose to regard them. The labourer set free from digging may want to spend his leisure, or part of it, in playing the piano, while the professional pianist may be only too glad to get out and dig at the potato patch. Hence the antithesis between work, as something intolerably tedious, and not-work, as something desirable, is false. The truth is that when a human being is not eating, drinking, sleeping, making love, talking, playing games or merely lounging about – and these things will not fill up a lifetime – he needs work and usually looks for it, though he may not call it work. Above the level of a third- or fourth-grade moron, life has got to be lived largely in terms of effort. For man is not, as the vulgarer hedonists seem to suppose, a kind of walking stomach; he has also got a hand, an eye and a brain. Cease to use your hands, and you have lopped off a huge chunk of your consciousness. And now consider again those half-dozen men who were digging the trench for the water-pipe. A machine has set them free from digging, and they are going to amuse themselves with something else – carpentering, for instance. But whatever they want to do, they will find that another machine has set them free from that. For in a fully mechanised world there would be no more need to carpenter, to cook, to mend motor-bicycles, etc., than there would be to dig. There is scarcely anything, from catching a whale to carving a cherry stone, that could not conceivably be done by machinery. The machine would even encroach upon the activities we now class as 'art'; it is doing so already, via the camera and the radio. Mechanise the world as fully as it might be mechanised, and whichever way you turn there will be some machine cutting you off from the chance of working – that is, of living.

At a first glance this might not seem to matter. Why should you not get on with your 'creative work' and disregard the machines that would do it for you? But it is not so simple as it sounds. Here am I, working eight hours a day in an insurance office; in my spare time I want to do something 'creative', so I choose to do a bit of carpentering – to make myself a table, for instance. Notice that from the very start there is a touch of artificiality about the whole business, for the factories can turn me out a far better table than I can make for myself. But even when I get to work on my table, it is not possible for me to feel towards it as the cabinet-maker of a hundred years ago felt towards his table, still less as Robinson Crusoe felt towards his. For before I start, most of the work has already been done for me by machinery. The tools I use demand the minimum of skill. I can get, for instance, planes which will cut out any moulding; the cabinet-maker of a hundred years ago would have had to do the work with chisel and gouge, which demanded real skill of eye and hand. The boards I buy are ready planed and the legs are ready turned by the lathe. I can even go to the wood-shop and buy all the parts of the table ready-made and only needing to be fitted together, my work being reduced to driving in a few pegs and using a piece of sandpaper. And if this is so at present, in the mechanised future it will be enormously more so. With the tools and materials available then, there will be no possibility of mistake, hence no room for skill. Making a table will be easier and duller than peeling a potato. In such circumstances it is nonsense to talk of 'creative work'. In any case the arts of the hand (which have got to be transmitted by apprenticeship) would long since have disappeared. Some of them have disappeared already, under the competition of the machine. Look round any country churchyard and see whether you can find a decently-cut tombstone later than 1820. The art, or rather the craft, of stonework has died out so completely that it would take centuries to revive it.

But it may be said, why not retain the machine *and* retain 'creative work'? Why not cultivate anachronisms as a spare-time hobby? Many people have played with this idea; it seems to solve with such beautiful ease the problems set by the machine. The citizen of Utopia, we are told, coming home from his daily two hours of turning a handle in the tomato-canning factory, will deliberately revert to a more primitive way of life and solace his creative instincts with a bit of fretwork, pottery-glazing or handloom-weaving. And why is this picture an absurdity – as it is, of course? Because of a principle that is not always recognised, though always acted upon: that so long as the machine is *there*, one is under an obligation to use it. No one draws water from the well when he can turn on the tap. [...] No human being ever wants to do anything in a more cumbrous way than is necessary. Hence the absurdity of that picture of Utopians saving their souls with fretwork. In a world where everything could be done by machinery, everything would be done by machinery. Deliberately to revert to primitive methods, to use archaic tools, to put silly little difficulties in your own way, would be a piece of dilettantism, of pretty-pretty arty and craftiness. It would be like solemnly sitting down to eat your dinner with stone implements. Revert to handwork in a machine age, and you are back in Ye Olde Tea Shoppe or the Tudor villa with the sham beams tacked to the wall.

The tendency of mechanical progress, then, is to frustrate the human need for effort and creation. It makes unnecessary and even impossible the activities of the eye and the hand. The apostle of 'progress' will sometimes declare that this does not matter, but you can usually drive him into a corner by pointing out the horrible lengths to which the process can be carried [...] There is really no reason why a human being should do more than eat, drink, sleep, breathe and procreate; *everything* else could be done for him by machinery. Therefore the logical end of mechanical progress is to reduce the human being to something resembling a brain in a bottle. That is the goal towards which we are already moving, though, of course, we have no intention of getting there; just as a man who drinks a bottle of whisky a day does not actually intend to get cirrhosis of the liver. The implied objective of 'progress' is – not *exactly*, perhaps, the brain in the bottle, but at any rate some frightful sub-human depth of softness and helplessness. [...] The machine has got to be accepted, but it is probably better to accept it rather as one accepts a drug – that is, grudgingly and suspiciously. Like a drug, the machine is useful, dangerous and habit-forming. The oftener one surrenders to it the tighter its grip becomes.

Like a drug, the machine is useful, dangerous and habit-forming. The oftener one surrenders to it the tighter its grip becomes.

'Human beings were trying to behave as human beings and not as cogs in the capitalist machine.'

From *Homage to Catalonia* (1938)

In the Lenin Barracks in Barcelona, the day before I joined the militia, I saw an Italian militiaman standing in front of the officers' table.

He was a tough-looking youth of twenty-five or -six, with reddish-yellow hair and powerful shoulders. His peaked leather cap was pulled fiercely over one eye. He was standing in profile to me, his chin on his breast, gazing with a puzzled frown at a map which one of the officers had open on the table. Something in his face deeply moved me. It was the face of a man who would commit murder and throw away his life for a friend – the kind of face you would expect in an Anarchist, though as likely as not he was a Communist. There were both candour and ferocity in it; also the pathetic reverence that illiterate people have for their supposed superiors. Obviously he could not make head or tail of the map; obviously he regarded map-reading as a stupendous intellectual feat. I hardly know why, but I have seldom seen anyone – any man, I mean – to whom I have taken such an immediate liking. While they were talking round the table some remark brought it out that I was a foreigner. The Italian raised his head and said quickly:

'*Italiano?*'

I answered in my bad Spanish: '*No, Inglés. Y tú?*'

'*Italiano.*'

As we went out he stepped across the room and gripped my hand very hard. Queer, the affection you can feel for a stranger! It was as though his spirit and mine had momentarily succeeded in bridging the gulf of language and tradition and meeting in utter intimacy. I hoped he liked me as well as I liked him. But I also knew that to retain my first impression of him I must not see him again; and needless to say I never did see him again. One was always making contacts of that kind in Spain.

I mention this Italian militiaman because he has stuck vividly in my memory. With his shabby uniform and fierce pathetic face he typifies for me the special atmosphere of that time. He is bound up with all my memories of that period of the war – the red flags in Barcelona, the gaunt trains full of shabby soldiers creeping to the front, the grey war-stricken towns further up the line, the muddy, ice-cold trenches in the mountains.

This was in late December, 1936, less than seven months ago as I write, and yet it is a period that has already receded into enormous distance. Later events have obliterated it much more completely than they have obliterated 1935, or 1905, for that matter. I had come to Spain with some notion of writing newspaper articles, but I had joined the militia almost immediately, because at that time and in that atmosphere it seemed the only conceivable thing to do. The Anarchists were still in virtual control of Catalonia and the revolution was still in full swing. To anyone who had been there since the beginning it probably seemed even in

December or January that the revolutionary period was ending; but when one came straight from England the aspect of Barcelona was something startling and overwhelming. It was the first time that I had ever been in a town where the working class was in the saddle. Practically every building of any size had been seized by the workers and was draped with red flags or with the red and black flag of the Anarchists; every wall was scrawled with the hammer and sickle and with the initials of the revolutionary parties; almost every church had been gutted and its images burnt. Churches here and there were being systematically demolished by gangs of workmen. Every shop and café had an inscription saying that it had been collectivized; even the bootblacks had been collectivized and their boxes painted red and black. Waiters and shop-walkers looked you in the face and treated you as an equal. Servile and even ceremonial forms of speech had temporarily disappeared. Nobody said '*Señor*' or '*Don*' or even '*Usted*'; everyone called everyone else '*Comrade*' and '*Thou*', and said

61

'*Salud!*' instead of '*Buenos días*'. Almost my first experience was receiving a lecture from an hotel manager for trying to tip a lift-boy. There were no private motor cars, they had all been commandeered, and all the trams and taxis and much of the other transport were painted red and black. The revolutionary posters were everywhere, flaming from the walls in clean reds and blues that made the few remaining advertisements look like daubs of mud. Down the Ramblas, the wide central artery of the town where crowds of people streamed constantly to and fro, the loudspeakers were bellowing revolutionary songs all day and far into the night. And it was the aspect of the crowds that was the queerest thing of all. In outward appearance it was a town in which the wealthy classes had practically ceased to exist. Except for a small number of women and foreigners there were no 'well-dressed' people at all. Practically everyone wore rough working-class clothes, or blue overalls or some variant of the militia uniform. All this was queer and moving. There was much in it that I did not understand, in some ways I did not even like it, but I recognized it immediately as a state of affairs worth fighting for. Also I believed that things were as they appeared, that this was really a workers' State and that the entire bourgeoisie had either fled, been killed, or voluntarily come over to the workers' side; I did not realize that great numbers of well-to-do bourgeois were simply lying low and disguising themselves as proletarians for the time being.

Together with all this there was something of the evil atmosphere of war. The town had a gaunt untidy look, roads and buildings were in poor repair, the streets at night were dimly lit for fear of air-raids, the shops were mostly shabby and half-empty. Meat was scarce and milk practically unobtainable, there was a shortage of coal, sugar, and petrol, and a really serious shortage of bread. Even at this period the bread-queues were often hundreds of yards long. Yet so far as one could judge the people were contented and hopeful. There was no unemployment, and the price of living was still extremely low; you saw very few conspicuously destitute people, and no beggars except the gipsies. Above all, there was a belief in the revolution and the future, a feeling of having suddenly emerged into an era of equality and freedom. Human beings were trying to behave as human beings and not as cogs in the capitalist machine. In the barbers' shops were Anarchist notices (the barbers were mostly Anarchists) solemnly explaining that barbers were no longer slaves.

There was a belief in the revolution and the future, a feeling of having suddenly emerged into an era of equality and freedom.

**'What *is* a road like Ellesmere Road?
Just a prison with the cells all in a row.'**

from *Coming Up for Air* (1939)

Do you know the road I live in – Ellesmere Road, West Bletchley? Even if you don't, you know fifty others exactly like it.

You know how these streets fester all over the inner-outer suburbs. Always the same. Long, long rows of little semi-detached houses – the numbers in Ellesmere Road run to 212 and ours is 191 – as much alike as council houses and generally uglier. The stucco front, the creosoted gate, the privet hedge, the green front door. The Laurels, The Myrtles, The Hawthorns, Mon Abri, Mon Repos, Belle Vue. At perhaps one house in fifty some anti-social type who'll probably end in the workhouse has painted his front door blue instead of green.

[A] sticky feeling round my neck had put me into a demoralised kind of mood. It's curious how it gets you down to have a sticky neck.

It seems to take all the bounce out of you, like when you suddenly discover in a public place that the sole of one of your shoes is coming off. I had no illusions about myself that morning. It was almost as if I could stand at a distance and watch myself coming down the road, with my fat red face and my false teeth and my vulgar clothes. A chap like me is incapable of looking like a gentleman. Even if you saw me at two hundred yards' distance you'd know immediately – not, perhaps, that I was in the insurance business, but that I was some kind of tout or salesman. The clothes I was wearing were practically the uniform of the tribe. Grey herringbone suit a bit the worse for wear, blue overcoat costing fifty shillings, bowler hat and no gloves. And I've got the look that's peculiar to people who sell things on commission, a kind of coarse brazen look. At my best moments, when I've got a new suit or when I'm smoking a cigar, I might pass for a bookie or a publican, and when things are very bad I might be touting vacuum cleaners, but at ordinary times you'd place me correctly. 'Five to ten quid a week', you'd say as

In every one of those little stucco boxes there's some poor bastard who's *never* free except when he's fast asleep and dreaming

soon as you saw me. Economically and socially I'm about at the average level of Ellesmere Road.

I had the street pretty much to myself. The men had bunked to catch the 8.21 and the women were fiddling with the gas-stoves. When you've time to look about you, and when you happen to be in the right mood, it's a thing that makes you laugh inside to walk down these streets in the inner-outer suburbs and to think of the lives that go on there. Because, after all, what *is* a road like Ellesmere Road? Just a prison with the cells all in a row. A line of semi-detached torture-chambers where the poor little five-to-ten-pound-a-weekers quake and shiver, every one of them with the boss twisting his tail and the wife riding him like the nightmare and the kids sucking his blood like leeches. There's a lot of rot talked about the sufferings of the working class. I'm not so sorry for the proles myself. Did you ever know a navvy who lay awake thinking about the sack? The prole suffers physically, but he's a free man when he isn't working. But in every one of those little stucco boxes there's some poor bastard who's *never* free except when he's fast asleep and dreaming that he's got the boss down the bottom of a well and is bunging lumps of coal at him.

'He understood that as a writer I might have a need for books which it was illegal to possess.'

'To Victor Gollancz'*
8 January 1940, typewritten

The Stores Wallington Nr. Baldock, HERTS.

Dear Mr Gollancz,
I cannot at this moment lend you 'Tropic of Cancer', because my copy has been seized. While I was writing my last book two detectives suddenly arrived at my house with orders from the public prosecutor to seize all books which I had 'received through the post'. A letter of mine addressed to the Obelisk Press had been seized and opened in the post. The police were only carrying out orders and

---

* Publisher's note: between 1933 and 1937, Victor Gollancz (1893–1967) had published Orwell's first five books.

71

were very nice about it, and even the public prosecutor wrote and said that he understood that as a writer I might have a need for books which it was illegal to possess. On these grounds he sent me back certain books, e.g. 'Lady Chatterley's Lover', but it appears that Miller's books have not been in print long enough to have become respectable. However, I know that Cyril Connolly has a copy of 'Tropic of Cancer'. He is down with flu at present, but when I can get in touch with him again I will borrow the book and pass it on to you.

As to your remarks on my book.★ I am glad you liked it. You are perhaps right in thinking I am over-pessimistic. It is quite possible that freedom of thought etc. may survive in an economically totalitarian society. We can't tell until a collectivised economy has been tried out in a western country. What worries me at present is the uncertainty as to whether

★ The manuscript of the collection of essays published under the title of one of them, *Inside the Whale*, 11 March 1940.

the ordinary people in countries like England grasp the difference between democracy and despotism well enough to want to defend their liberties. One can't tell until they see themselves menaced in some quite unmistakeable manner. The intellectuals who are at present pointing out that democracy and fascism are the same thing etc. depress me horribly. However, perhaps when the pinch comes the common people will turn out to be more intelligent than the clever ones. I certainly hope so.

Yours sincerely
Eric Blair

'A land of snobbery and privilege, ruled largely by the old and silly.'

from *The Lion and the Unicorn*
(February 1941)

England is the most class-ridden country under the sun. It is a land of snobbery and privilege, ruled largely by the old and silly. But in any calculation about it one has got to take into account its emotional unity, the tendency of nearly all its inhabitants to feel alike and act together in moments of supreme crisis. It is the only great country in Europe that is not obliged to drive hundreds of thousands of its nationals into exile or the concentration camp. At this moment, after a year of war, newspapers and pamphlets abusing the Government, praising the enemy and clamouring for surrender are being sold on the streets, almost without interference. And this is less from a respect for freedom of speech than from a simple perception that these things don't matter. It is safe to let a paper like *Peace News* be sold, because it is certain that ninety-five per cent of the population will never want to read it. The nation is bound together by an invisible chain. At any normal time the ruling class will rob, mismanage, sabotage, lead us into the muck; but let popular opinion really make itself heard, let them get a tug from below that they cannot avoid feeling, and it is difficult for them not to respond. The left-wing writers who denounce the whole of the ruling class as 'pro-Fascist' are grossly over-simplifying. Even among the inner clique of politicians who brought us to our present pass, it is doubtful whether there were any conscious traitors. The corruption that happens in England is seldom of that kind. Nearly always it is more in the nature of self-deception, of the right hand not knowing what the left hand doeth. And being unconscious, it is limited. One sees this at its most obvious in the English Press. Is the English press honest or dishonest? At normal times it is deeply dishonest. All the papers that matter live off their advertisements, and the advertisers exercise an indirect censorship over news. Yet I do not suppose there is one paper in England that can be straightforwardly bribed with hard cash. In the France of the Third Republic all but a very few of the newspapers could notoriously be bought over the counter like so many pounds of cheese. Public life in England has never been openly scandalous. It has not reached the pitch of disintegration at which humbug can be dropped.

England is not the jewelled isle of Shakespeare's much-quoted passage, nor is it the inferno depicted by Dr. Goebbels. More than either it resembles a family, a rather stuffy Victorian family, with not many black sheep in it but with all its cupboards bursting with skeletons. It has rich relations who have to be kow-towed to and poor relations who are horribly sat upon, and there is a deep conspiracy of silence about the source of the family income. It is a family in which the young are generally thwarted and most of the power is in the hands of irresponsible uncles and bedridden aunts.

The nation is bound together by an invisible chain.

Still, it is a family. It has its private language and its common memories, and at the approach of an enemy it closes its ranks. A family with the wrong members in control – that, perhaps, is as near as one can come to describing England in a phrase.

[...] It must be admitted that so long as things were peaceful the methods of the British ruling class served them well enough. Their own people manifestly tolerated them. However unjustly England might be organized, it was at any rate not torn by class warfare or haunted by secret police. The Empire was peaceful as no area of comparable size has ever been. Throughout its vast extent, nearly a quarter of the earth, there were fewer armed men than would be found necessary by a minor Balkan state. As people to live under, and looking at them merely from a liberal, *negative* standpoint, the British ruling class had their points. They were preferable to the truly modern men, the Nazis and Fascists. But it had long been obvious that they would be helpless against any serious attack from the outside.

They could not struggle against Nazism or Fascism, because they could not understand them. Neither could they have struggled against Communism, if Communism had been a serious force in western Europe. To understand Fascism they would have had to study the theory of Socialism, which would have forced them to realize that the economic system by which they lived was unjust, inefficient and out of date. But it was exactly this fact that they had trained themselves never to face. They dealt with Fascism as the cavalry generals of 1914 dealt with the machine gun – by ignoring it. After years of aggression and massacres, they had grasped only one fact, that Hitler and Mussolini were hostile to Communism. Therefore, it was argued, they *must* be friendly to the British dividend-drawer. Hence the truly frightening spectacle of Conservative M.P.s wildly cheering the news that British ships, bringing food to the Spanish Republican government, had been bombed by Italian aeroplanes. Even when they had begun to grasp that Fascism was dangerous, its essentially revolutionary nature, the huge military effort it was capable of making, the sort of tactics it would use, were quite beyond their comprehension. At the time of the Spanish civil war, anyone with as much political knowledge as can be acquired from a sixpenny pamphlet on Socialism knew that if Franco won, the result would be strategically disastrous for England; and yet generals and admirals who had given their lives to the study of war were unable to grasp this fact. This vein of political ignorance runs right through English official life, through Cabinet ministers, ambassadors, consuls, judges, magistrates, policemen. The policeman who arrests the 'Red' does not understand the theories the 'Red' is preaching; if he did, his own position as bodyguard of the monied class might seem less pleasant to him. There is reason to think that even military espionage is hopelessly hampered by ignorance of the new economic doctrines and the ramifications of the underground parties.

The British ruling class were not altogether wrong in thinking that Fascism was on their side. It is a fact that any rich man, unless he is a Jew, has less to fear from Fascism than from either Communism or democratic Socialism. One ought never to forget this, for nearly the whole of German and Italian propaganda is designed to cover it up. The natural instinct of men like [Sir John] Simon, [Sir Samuel] Hoare, [Neville] Chamberlain, etc., was to come to an agreement with Hitler. But – and here the peculiar feature of English life that I have spoken of, the deep sense of national solidarity, comes in – they could only do so by breaking up the Empire and selling their own people into semi-slavery. A truly corrupt class would have done this without hesitation, as in France. But things had not gone that distance in England. Politicians who would make cringing speeches about 'the duty of loyalty to our conquerors' are hardly to be found in English public life. Tossed to and fro between their incomes and their principles, it was impossible that men like Chamberlain should do anything but make the worst of both worlds.

One thing that has always shown that the English ruling class are *morally* fairly sound, is that in time of war they are ready enough to get themselves killed. Several dukes, earls and what-not were killed in the recent campaign in Flanders. That could not happen if these people were the cynical scoundrels that they are sometimes declared to be. It is important not to misunderstand their motives, or one cannot predict their actions. What is to be expected of them is not treachery or physical cowardice, but stupidity, unconscious sabotage, an infallible instinct for doing the wrong thing. They are not wicked, or not altogether wicked; they are merely unteachable. Only when their money and power are gone will the younger among them begin to grasp what century they are living in.

'Freedom may be an illusion'
from 'Will Freedom Die with Capitalism?'★
The Left News, April 1941

It is not claimed by Socialists that the change-over to a collectivist economy will make human life happier, easier or even freer *immediately*. On the contrary, the transition may make life very nearly unbearable for a long period, perhaps for hundreds of years. There is a certain goal that we have got to reach – cannot help reaching, ultimately – and the way to it may lead through some dreadful places. What Socialists of, I should say, nearly all schools believe is that the destiny and therefore the true happiness of man lies in a

---

★ Publisher's note: Orwell's article was written in response to a letter from Douglas Ede, of Withersfield, Suffolk, to the Editor of *The Left News*: 'I am sure many of your readers are like me, and feel that good intentions are not enough. Maybe your policy is an alternate Democracy to capitalistic Democracy, AND yet not communistic or fascist, if so you had better define it more clearly'.

society of pure communism, that is to say a society in which all human beings are more or less equal, in which no one has the power to oppress another, in which economic motives have ceased to operate, in which men are governed by love and curiosity and not by greed and fear. That is our destiny, and there is no escaping it; but *how* we reach it, and *how soon*, depends on ourselves. Socialism – centralised ownership of the means of production, plus political democracy – is the necessary next step towards communism, just as capitalism was the necessary next step after feudalism. It is not in itself the final objective, and I think we ought to guard against assuming that *as a system to live under* it will be greatly preferable to democratic capitalism.

[...] There is no reason for thinking that the West will imitate the East. When people speak of the West, or Western civilisation, they mean a ring of states fringing on the North Atlantic, Scandinavia, the Low Countries, France, Britain and North America. These states have enough in common to be thought of as a single culture. All of them were infected by the ideas of the French Revolution, all of them have developed parliamentary democracies which were inefficient but which did act as a check on political adventurers, and all of them have had a high enough standard of living to allow independent labour movements to develop. The two biggest of them have been saved by their maritime position from foreign invasion and the rule of armies. Most important of all, a belief in the *value* of bourgeois Democracy is widespread in all these countries, and more among the common people than among their rulers. Freedom may be an illusion, but you could not, in England, induce large numbers of young men to march up and down proclaiming 'We spit upon Freedom,' and that fact is symptomatically important. The enemies of Western civilisation are fond of pointing out that the comparative peacefulness and decency of life in the democracies are simply the reflection of a high national income, which for a hundred years past has been based largely on coloured labour. This is true, but it is rather like saying 'This field is only more fertile than that because it was manured last year.' Our scruples are not less real because we have bought them with the blood of Indian coolies. A hatred of civil violence and a respect for freedom of speech are definite factors in Western life, and they are not likely to vanish overnight, even if our standard of living drops to that of Eastern Europe. Men's beliefs are not so crudely dependent on material circumstances as to alter from day to day, or even from year to year. A professor of science wrecked on a desert island may be reduced to the condition of a savage, but he does not become a savage. He does not start believing that the sun goes round the earth, for instance. When our revolution is accomplished our social and economic structure will be totally different, but we shall retain many of the habits of thought and behaviour that we learned in an earlier age. Nations do not easily wipe out their past. There is no question of saving capitalist Democracy, it is disappearing, but that is not to say that one Monday morning we shall wake up to a world of slogans and rubber truncheons. I think the answer to Mr. Ede's query must be that if we can bring our revolution about it will be comparatively speaking a bloodless one, and that many features of capitalist Democracy, whose disappearance he rightly dreads, will be able to survive it.

All depends on the 'if.' We have to keep our destiny in our own hands, which implies waging the 'war on two fronts.' I have said earlier that we shall emerge from this war either Socialist, nazified by conquest, or victorious but with a brand of fascism peculiar to ourselves. And it is doubtful whether the third alternative practically exists. One striking thing about this war has been the failure of the British ruling-class to develop a genuinely Fascist outlook. In spite of a certain amount of will to do so, they seem not to possess either the intelligence, the political understanding or the simple wickedness to learn totalitarian methods. Of course England is still a class-ridden country, and the offensive contrast of wealth and poverty exists everywhere amid the bombs; but that is plutocracy, a very different thing from fascism. And of course there is curtailment of the rights of labour, press censorship, political persecution of a petty kind, a general diminution of liberty. But that is war. One has to compare the behaviour of the British Government not with some impossible ideal but with that of *any* government at war, whatever its colour. The Spanish Republican Government, for instance, from the very beginning of the civil war, outraged every principle of Democracy far more grossly than our own Government has done, or, I should say, than any British Conservative Government would dare to do. The clumsy, ineffectual chasing of the People's Convention is not the act of Fascists; it is the act of stupid plutocrats who would rather like to introduce totalitarian methods but do not know how. Of course we have to be on our guard against these people, and to lever them out when the opportunity arises, but less because they are likely to consolidate their own power than because they will lose the war for us if they are left in control.

When the opportunity for a shift of power will arise, I do not know. It does not exist at this moment; I think it existed after Dunkirk.

And at this particular moment I do not see what one can do, politically, except to spread as widely as possible the following three ideas.

(i) Human progress may be held up for centuries unless we can eliminate Hitler, which means that Britain must win the war.

(ii) The war cannot be won unless the first steps towards socialism are taken.

(iii) No revolution in England has a chance of success unless it takes account of England's past.

But what our 'new Utopia,' as Mr. Ede calls it, will be like in its first stage we cannot tell. We do not know how it will be reached, whether fairly easily and by the willing act of the majority of the people, or slowly and painfully, through dictatorship and civil war. I have merely given reasons for thinking that revolution in England might be less bloody and disappointing than elsewhere. There is no certainty that the first phase of socialism will be 'better,' from a hedonistic point of view, than democratic capitalism. But we cannot take account of that, because we can only consider the possibilities that exist. The one certain thing about this war is that we shall not end up where we began. To say that since capitalist Democracy has its points it would be better to retain it in toto, is as though a baby should say that since lying in a cradle is a very pleasant thing, it would be better to remain a baby all your life. No such thing can happen, and to wish for the impossible, even the impossible good, is inherently reactionary.

'Take away freedom of Speech, and the creative faculties dry up.'

'As I Please', 22
Tribune, 28 April 1944

On the night in 1940 when the big ack-ack barrage was fired over London for the first time,★ I was in Piccadilly Circus when the guns opened up, and I fled into the Café Royal to take cover. Among the crowd inside a good-looking, well-made youth of about twenty-five was making somewhat of a nuisance of himself with a copy of *Peace News*, which he was forcing upon the attention of everyone at the neighbouring tables. I got into conversation with him, and the conversation went something like this:

The youth: 'I tell you, it'll all be over by Christmas. There's obviously going to be a

---

★ 10 September 1940.

compromise peace. I'm pinning my faith to Sir Samuel Hoare. It's degrading company to be in, I admit, but still Hoare is on our side. So long as Hoare's in Madrid, there's always hope of a sell-out.'

Orwell: 'What about all these preparations that they're making against invasion – the pill-boxes that they're building everywhere, the L.D.V.s,* and so forth?'

The youth: 'Oh, that merely means that they're getting ready to crush the working class when the Germans get here. I suppose some of them might be fools enough to try to resist, but Churchill and the Germans between them won't take long to settle them. Don't worry, it'll soon be over.'

Orwell: 'Do you really want to see your children grow up Nazis?'

The youth: 'Nonsense! You don't suppose the Germans are going to encourage Fascism in this country, do you? They don't want to breed

---

* Local Defence Volunteers.

up a race of warriors to fight against them. Their object will be to turn us into slaves. They'll encourage every pacifist movement they can lay hands on. That's why I'm a pacifist. They'll encourage people like me.'

Orwell: 'And shoot people like me?'

The youth: 'That would be just too bad.'

Orwell: 'But why are you so anxious to remain alive?'

The youth: 'So that I can get on with my work, of course.'

It had come out in the conversation that the youth was a painter – whether good or bad I do not know; but, at any rate, sincerely interested in painting and quite ready to face poverty in pursuit of it. As a painter, he would probably have been somewhat better off under a German occupation than a writer or journalist would be. But still, what he said contained a very dangerous fallacy, now very widespread in the countries where totalitarianism has not actually established itself.

The fallacy is to believe that under a dictatorial government you can be free *inside*. Quite a number of people console themselves with this thought, now that totalitarianism in one form or another is visibly on the up-grade in every part of the world. Out in the street the loudspeakers bellow, the flags flutter from the rooftops, the police with their tommy-guns prowl to and fro, the face of the Leader, four feet wide, glares from every hoarding; but up in the attics the secret enemies of the regime can record their thoughts in perfect freedom – that is the idea, more or less. And many people are under the impression that this is going on now in Germany and other dictatorial countries.

Why is this idea false? I pass over the fact that modern dictatorships don't, in fact, leave the loopholes that the old-fashioned despotisms did; and also the probable weakening of the *desire* for intellectual liberty owing to totalitarian methods of education. The greatest mistake is to imagine that the human being is an autonomous individual. The secret freedom

The fallacy is to believe that under a dictatorial government you can be free *inside*.

which you can supposedly enjoy under a despotic Government is nonsense, because your thoughts are never entirely your own. Philosophers, writers, artists, even scientists, not only need encouragement and an audience, they need constant stimulation from other people. It is almost impossible to think without talking. If Defoe had really lived on a desert island he could not have written *Robinson Crusoe*, nor would he have wanted to. Take away freedom of Speech, and the creative faculties dry up. Had the Germans really got to England my acquaintance of the Café Royal would soon have found his painting deteriorating, even if the Gestapo had let him alone. And when the lid is taken off Europe, I believe one of the things that will surprise us will be to find how little worthwhile writing of any kind – even such things as diaries, for instance – have been produced in secret under the dictators.

'No animal in England is free.'

from *Animal Farm* (1945)

'Now, comrades, what is the nature of this life of ours? Let us face it, our lives are miserable, laborious and short. We are born, we are given just so much food as will keep the breath in our bodies, and those of us who are capable of it are forced to work to the last atom of our strength; and the very instant that our usefulness has come to an end we are slaughtered with hideous cruelty. No animal in England knows the meaning of happiness or leisure after he is a year old. No animal in England is free. The life of an animal is misery and slavery: that is the plain truth.

'But is this simply part of the order of Nature? Is it because this land of ours is so poor that it cannot afford a decent life to those who dwell upon it? No, comrades, a thousand times no! The soil of England is fertile, its climate is good, it is capable of affording food in abundance to an enormously greater number of animals than now

inhabit it. This single farm of ours would support a dozen horses, twenty cows, hundreds of
sheep – and all of them living in a comfort and
a dignity that are now almost beyond our imag-
ining. Why then do we continue in this miserable
condition? Because nearly the whole of the produce of our labour is stolen from us by human
beings. There, comrades, is the answer to all our
problems. It is summed up in a single word –
Man. Man is the only real enemy we have.
Remove Man from the scene, and the root cause
of hunger and overwork is abolished for ever.

'Man is the only creature that consumes without producing. He does not give milk, he does
not lay eggs, he is too weak to pull the plough,
he cannot run fast enough to catch rabbits. Yet he
is lord of all the animals. He sets them to work,
he gives back to them the bare minimum that
will prevent them from starving, and the rest he
keeps for himself. Our labour tills the soil, our
dung fertilises it, and yet there is not one of us
that owns more than his bare skin. [...]

'Is it not crystal clear, then, comrades, that all
the evils of this life of ours spring from the

'Is it not crystal clear, then, comrades, that all the evils of this life of ours spring from the tyranny of human beings?'

tyranny of human beings? Only get rid of Man, and the produce of our labour would be our own. Almost overnight we could become rich and free. What then must we do? Why, work night and day, body and soul, for the overthrow of the human race! That is my message to you, comrades: Rebellion!'

'They had come to a time when no one dared to speak his mind.'

From *Animal Farm* (1945)

Four days later, in the late afternoon, Napoleon ordered all the animals to assemble in the yard. When they were all gathered together Napoleon emerged from the farmhouse, wearing both his medals (for he had recently awarded himself 'Animal Hero, First Class' and 'Animal Hero, Second Class'), with his nine huge dogs frisking round him and uttering growls that sent shivers down all the animals' spines. They all cowered silently in their places, seeming to know in advance that some terrible thing was about to happen.

Napoleon stood sternly surveying his audience; then he uttered a high-pitched whimper. Immediately the dogs bounded forward, seized four of the pigs by the ear and dragged them, squealing with pain and terror, to Napoleon's feet. The pigs' ears were bleeding, the dogs had tasted blood and for a few moments they appeared to go quite mad. To the amazement of everybody three of them flung themselves upon Boxer. Boxer saw them coming and put out his great hoof, caught a dog in mid-air and pinned him to the ground. The dog shrieked for mercy and the other two fled with their tails between their legs. Boxer looked at Napoleon to know whether he should crush the dog to death or let it go. Napoleon appeared to change countenance, and sharply ordered Boxer to let the dog go, whereat Boxer lifted his hoof, and the dog slunk away, bruised and howling.

Presently the tumult died down. The four pigs waited, trembling, with guilt written on every line of their countenances. Napoleon now called upon them to confess their crimes. They were the same four pigs as had protested when Napoleon abolished the Sunday Meetings. Without any further prompting they confessed that they had been secretly in touch with Snowball ever since his expulsion, that they had collaborated with him in destroying the windmill, and that they had entered into an agreement with him to hand over Animal Farm to Mr Frederick. They added that Snowball had privately admitted to them that he had been Jones's secret agent for years past. When they had finished their confession the dogs promptly tore their throats out, and in a terrible voice Napoleon demanded whether any other animals had anything to confess.

The three hens who had been the ringleaders in the attempted rebellion over the eggs now came forward and stated that Snowball had appeared to them in a dream and incited them to disobey Napoleon's orders. They too were slaughtered. Then a goose came forward and confessed to having secreted six ears of corn during the last year's harvest and eaten them in the night. Then a sheep confessed to having urinated in the drinking pool – urged to do this, so she said, by Snowball – and two other sheep confessed to having murdered an old ram, an especially devoted follower of Napoleon, by chasing him round and round a bonfire when he was suffering from a cough. They were all slain on the spot. And so the tale of confessions and executions went on, until there was a pile of corpses lying before Napoleon's feet and the air was heavy with the smell of blood, which had been unknown there since the expulsion of Jones.

When it was all over, the remaining animals, except for the pigs and dogs, crept away in a body. They were shaken and miserable. They did not know which was more shocking – the treachery of the animals who had leagued themselves with Snowball, or the cruel retribution they had just witnessed. In the old days there had often been scenes of bloodshed equally terrible, but it seemed to all of them that it was far worse now that it was happening among themselves. Since Jones had left the farm, until today, no animal had killed another animal. Not even a rat had been killed. They had made their way onto the little knoll where the half-finished windmill stood, and with one accord they all lay down as though huddling together for warmth – Clover, Muriel,

Benjamin, the cows, the sheep and a whole flock of geese and hens – everyone, indeed, except the cat, who had suddenly disappeared just before Napoleon ordered the animals to assemble. For some time nobody spoke. Only Boxer remained on his feet. He fidgeted to and fro, swishing his long black tail against his sides and occasionally uttering a little whinny of surprise. Finally he said:

'I do not understand it. I would not have believed that such things could happen on our farm. It must be due to some fault in ourselves. The solution, as I see it, is to work harder. From now onwards I shall get up a full hour earlier in the mornings.'

And he moved off at his lumbering trot and made for the quarry. Having got there he collected two successive loads of stone and dragged them to the windmill before retiring for the night.

The animals huddled about Clover, not speaking. The knoll where they were lying gave them a wide prospect across the country-side. Most of Animal Farm was within their view – the long pasture stretching down to the main road, the hayfield, the spinney, the drinking pool, the ploughed fields where the young wheat was thick and green, and the red roofs of the farm buildings with the smoke curling from the chimneys. Never had the farm – and with a kind of surprise they remembered that it was their own farm, every inch of it their own property – appeared to the animals so desirable a place. As Clover looked down the hillside her eyes filled with tears. If she could have spoken her thoughts, it would have been to say that this was not what they had aimed at when they had set themselves years ago to work for the overthrow of the human race. These scenes of terror and slaughter were not what they had looked forward to on that night when old Major first stirred them to rebellion. If she herself had had any picture of the future, it had been of a society of animals set free from hunger and whip, all equal, each working according to his capacity, the strong protecting the weak, as she had protected the lost brood of ducklings with her foreleg on the night of Major's speech. Instead – she did not know why – they had come to a time when no one dared to speak his mind, when fierce, growling dogs roamed everywhere, and when you had to watch your comrades torn to pieces after confessing to shocking crimes. There was no thought of rebellion or disobedience in her mind. She knew that even as things were they were far better off than they had been in the days of Jones, and that before all else it was needful to prevent the return of the human beings. Whatever happened she would remain faithful, work hard, carry out the orders that were given to her, and accept the leadership of Napoleon. But still, it was not for this that she and all the other animals had hoped and toiled. It was not for this that they had built the windmill and faced the pellets of Jones's gun. Such were her thoughts, though she lacked the words to express them.

At last, feeling this to be in some way a substitute for the words she was unable to find, she began to sing 'Beasts of England'.★ The other animals sitting round her took it up, and they sang it three times over – very tunefully, but slowly and mournfully, in a way they had never sung it before.

They had just finished singing it for the third time when Squealer, attended by two dogs, approached them with the air of having something important to say. He announced that, by a special decree of Comrade Napoleon, 'Beasts of England' had been abolished. From now onwards it was forbidden to sing it.

The animals were taken aback.

'Why?' cried Muriel.

'It is no longer needed, comrade,' said Squealer stiffly. '"Beasts of England" was the song of the Rebellion. But the Rebellion is now completed. The execution of the traitors

---

★ 'Beasts of England' was the animals' stirring anthem, composed by the old pig Major, and spoke of a time when 'Tyrant Man shall be o'erthrown, / And the fruitful fields of England / Shall be trod by beasts alone ... Rings shall vanish from our noses, / And the harness from our back, / Bit and spur shall rust forever, / Cruel whips no more shall crack.'

this afternoon was the final act. The enemy both external and internal has been defeated. In "Beasts of England" we expressed our longing for a better society in days to come. But that society has now been established. Clearly this song has no longer any purpose.'

Frightened though they were, some of the animals might possibly have protested, but at this moment the sheep set up their usual bleating of 'Four legs good, two legs bad', which went on for several minutes and put an end to the discussion.

So 'Beasts of England' was heard no more. In its place Minimus, the poet, had composed another song which began:

> *Animal Farm, Animal Farm,*
> *Never through me shalt thou come to harm!*

and this was sung every Sunday morning after the hoisting of the flag. But somehow neither the words nor the tune ever seemed to the animals to come up to 'Beasts of England'.

'There is now a widespread tendency to argue that one can only defend democracy by totalitarian methods.'

from 'Publication of *Animal Farm*;
"The Freedom of the Press"'
London, 17 August 1945
New York, 26 August 1946

One of the peculiar phenomena of our time is the renegade Liberal. Over and above the familiar Marxist claim that 'bourgeois liberty' is an illusion, there is now a widespread tendency to argue that one can only defend democracy by totalitarian methods. If one loves democracy, the argument runs, one must crush its enemies by no matter what means. And who are its enemies? It always appears that they are not only those who attack it openly and consciously, but those who 'objectively' endanger it by spreading mistaken doctrines. In other words, defending democracy involves destroying all independence of thought. This argument was used, for instance, to justify the Russian purges. The most ardent Russophile hardly believed that all of the victims were guilty of all the things they were accused of: but by holding heretical opinions they 'objectively' harmed the régime, and therefore it was quite right not only to massacre them but to discredit them by false accusations. The same argument was used to justify the quite conscious lying that went on in the leftwing press about the Trotsky-ists and other Republican minorities in the Spanish civil war. And it was used again as a rea-son for yelping against *habeas corpus* when [Oswald] Mosley was released in 1943.

These people don't see that if you encourage totalitarian methods, the time may come when they will be used against you instead of for you. Make a habit of imprisoning Fascists without trial, and perhaps the process won't stop at Fas-cists. Soon after the suppressed *Daily Worker* had been reinstated, I was lecturing to a working-men's college in South London. The audience were working-class and lower-middle class intellectuals – the same sort of audience that one used to meet at Left Book Club branches. The lecture had touched on the freedom of the press, and at the end, to my astonishment, several questioners stood up and asked me: Did I not think that the lifting of the ban on the *Daily Worker* was a great mistake? When asked why, they said that it was a paper of doubtful loyalty and ought not to be tolerated in war time. I found myself defending the *Daily Worker*, which has gone out of its way to libel me more than once. But where had these people learned this essentially totalitarian outlook? Pretty certainly they had learned it from the Communists themselves! Tolerance and decency are deeply rooted in England, but they are not indestructible, and they have to be kept alive partly by conscious effort. The result of preaching totalitarian doctrines is to weaken the instinct by means of which free peoples know what is or is not dangerous. The case of Mosley illustrates this. In 1940 it was perfectly right to intern Mosley, whether or not he had committed any technical crime. We were fighting for our lives and could not allow a possible quisling to go free. To keep him shut up, without trial, in 1943 was an outrage. The general failure to see this was a bad symptom, though it is true that the agitation against Mosley's release was partly factitious and partly a rationalisation of other discontents. But how much of the present slide towards Fascist ways of thought is traceable to the 'anti-Fascism' of the past ten years and the unscrupulousness it has entailed?

It is important to realise that the current Russomania is only a symptom of the general weakening of the western liberal tradition. Had the MOI chipped in and definitely vetoed the publication of this book [i.e. *Animal Farm*], the bulk of the English intelligentsia would have seen nothing disquieting in this. Uncritical loyalty to the USSR happens to be the current orthodoxy, and where the supposed interests of the USSR are involved they are willing to tolerate not only censorship but the deliberate falsification of history. To name one instance. At the death of John Reed, the author of *Ten Days that Shook the World* – a first-hand account of the early days of the Russian Revolution – the copyright of the book passed into the hands of the British Communist Party, to whom I believe Reed had bequeathed it. Some years later the British Communists, having destroyed the original edition of the book as completely as they could, issued a garbled version from which they had eliminated mentions of Trotsky and also omitted the introduction written by Lenin. If a radical intelligentsia had still existed in Britain, this act of forgery would have been exposed and denounced in every literary paper in the country. As it was there was little or no protest. To many English intellectuals it seemed quite a natural thing to do. And this tolerance or plain dishonesty means much more than that admiration of Russia happens to be fashionable at this moment. Quite possibly that particular fashion will not last. For all I know, by the time this book is published my view of the Soviet régime may be the generally-accepted one. But what use would that be in itself? To exchange one orthodoxy for another is not necessarily an advance. The enemy is the gramophone mind, whether or not one agrees with the record that is being played at the moment.

I am well acquainted with all the arguments against freedom of thought and speech – the arguments which claim that it cannot exist, and the arguments which claim that it ought not to. I answer simply that they don't convince me and that our civilisation over a period of four hundred years has been founded on the opposite notion. For quite a decade past I have believed that the existing Russian régime is a mainly evil thing, and I claim the right to say so, in spite of the fact that we are allies with the USSR in a war which I want to see won. If I had to choose a text to justify myself, I should choose the line from Milton:

By the known rules of ancient liberty.

The word *ancient* emphasises the fact that intellectual freedom is a deep-rooted tradition without which our characteristic western culture could only doubtfully exist. From that tradition many of our intellectuals are visibly turning away. They have accepted the principle that a book should be published or suppressed, praised or damned, not on its merits but according to political expediency. And others who do not actually hold this view assent to it from sheer cowardice. An example of this is the failure of the numerous and vocal English pacifists to raise their voices against the prevalent worship of Russian militarism. According to those pacifists, all violence is evil, and they have urged us at every stage of the war to give in or at least to make a compromise peace. But how many of them have ever suggested that war is also evil when it is waged by the Red Army? Apparently the Russians have a right to defend themselves, whereas for us to do [so] is a deadly sin. One can only explain this contradiction in one way: that is, by a cowardly desire to keep in with the bulk of the intelligentsia, whose patriotism is directed towards the USSR rather than towards Britain. I know that the English intelligentsia have plenty of reason for their timidity and dishonesty, indeed I know by heart the arguments by which they justify themselves. But at least let us have no more nonsense about defending liberty against Fascism. If liberty means anything at all it means the right to tell people what they do not want

If liberty means anything
at all it means the right
to tell people what they
do not want to hear.

to hear. The common people still vaguely sub-
scribe to that doctrine and act on it. In our
country – it is not the same in all countries: it
was not so in republican France, and it is not so
in the USA today – it is the liberals who fear
liberty and the intellectuals who want to do
dirt on the intellect: it is to draw attention to
that fact that I have written this preface.

'The relative freedom which we enjoy depends on public opinion.'

'Freedom of the Park'
Tribune, 7 December 1945

A few weeks ago, five people who were selling papers outside Hyde Park were arrested by the police for obstruction. When taken before the magistrate they were all found guilty, four of them being bound over for six months and the other sentenced to forty shillings' fine or a month's imprisonment. He preferred to serve his term, so I suppose he is still in jail at this moment.

The papers these people were selling were *Peace News, Forward* and *Freedom*, besides other kindred literature. *Peace News* is the organ of the Peace Pledge Union, *Freedom* (till recently called *War Commentary*) is that of the Anarchists: as for *Forward*, its politics defy definition, but at any rate it is violently Left. The magistrate, in passing sentence, stated that he was not influenced by the nature of the literature that was being sold: he was concerned merely with the fact of obstruction, and that this offence had technically been committed.

This raises several important points. To begin with, how does the law stand on the subject? As far as I can discover, selling newspapers in the street is technically obstruction, at any rate if you fail to move on when the police tell you to. So it would be legally possible for any policeman who felt like it to arrest any newsboy for selling the *Evening News*. Obviously this doesn't happen, so that the enforcement of the law depends on the discretion of the police.

And what makes the police decide to arrest one man rather than another? However it may have been with the magistrate, I find it hard to believe that in this case the police were not influenced by political considerations. It is a bit too much of a coincidence that they should have picked on people selling just those papers. If they had also arrested someone who was selling *Truth*, or the *Tablet*, or the *Spectator*, or even the *Church Times*, their impartiality would be easier to believe in.

The British police are not like a continental gendarmerie or Gestapo, but I do not think one maligns them in saying that, in the past, they have been unfriendly to Left-wing activities. They have generally shown a tendency to side with those whom they regarded as the defenders of private property. There were some scandalous cases at the time of the Mosley disturbances. At the only big Mosley meeting I ever attended, the police collaborated with the Blackshirts in 'keeping order,' in a way in which they certainly would not have collaborated with Socialists or Communists. Till quite recently 'red' and 'illegal' were almost synonymous, and it was always the seller of, say, the *Daily Worker*, never the seller of, say, the *Daily Telegraph*, who was moved on and generally harassed. Apparently it can be the same, at any rate at moments, under a Labour government.

A thing I would like to know – it is a thing we hear very little about – is what changes are made in the administrative personnel when there has been a change of government. Does the police officer who has a vague notion that

'Socialism' means something against the law carry on just the same when the government itself is Socialist? It is a sound principle that the official should have no party affiliations, should serve successive governments faithfully and should not be victimised for his political opinions. Still, no government can afford to leave its enemies in key positions, and when Labour is in undisputed power for the first time – and therefore when it is taking over an administration formed by Conservatives – it clearly must make sufficient changes to prevent sabotage. The official, even when friendly to the government in power, is all too conscious that he is a permanency and can frustrate the short-lived Ministers whom he is supposed to serve.

When a Labour Government takes over, I wonder what happens to Scotland Yard Special Branch? To Military Intelligence? To the Consular Service? To the various colonial administrations – and so on and so forth? We are not told, but such symptoms as there are do not suggest that any very extensive reshuffling is going on. We are still represented abroad by the same ambassadors, and B.B.C. censorship seems to have the same subtly reactionary colour that it always had. The B.B.C. claims, of course, to be both independent and non-political. I was told once that its 'line,' if any, was to represent the Left wing of the government in power. But that was in the days of the Churchill Government. If it represents the Left Wing of the present Government, I have not noticed the fact.

However, the main point of this episode is that the sellers of newspapers and pamphlets should be interfered with at all. Which particular minority is singled out – whether Pacifists, Communists, Anarchists, Jehovah's Witness or the Legion of Christian Reformers who recently declared Hitler to be Jesus Christ – is a secondary matter. It is of symptomatic importance that these people should have been arrested at that particular spot. You are not allowed to sell literature inside Hyde Park, but for many years past it has been usual for the paper-sellers to station themselves just outside the gates and distribute literature connected with the open-air meetings a hundred yards away. Every kind of publication has been sold there without interference.

As for the meetings inside the Park, they are one of the minor wonders of the world. At different times I have listened there to Indian nationalists, Temperance reformers, Communists, Trotskyists, the S.P.G.B.,★ the Catholic Evidence Society, Freethinkers, vegetarians, Mormons, the Salvation Army, the Church Army, and a large variety of plain lunatics, all taking their turn at the rostrum in an orderly way and receiving a fairly good-humoured hearing from the crowd. Granted that Hyde Park is a special area, a sort of Alsatia† where outlawed opinions are permitted to walk – still, there are very few countries in the world where

---

★ The Socialist Party of Great Britain, a Marxist organisation having no connection with the Labour Party.

† The French edition of *Down and Out in Paris and London* (1935) had a footnote by Orwell explaining Alsatia. This read (translated into English): 'A name once given to the district of Whitefriars, which was, in the seventeenth century, a regular refuge for all kinds of wrongdoers by virtue of a right of sanctuary which was finally abolished in 1697'.

you can see a similar spectacle. I have known continental Europeans, long before Hitler seized power, come away from Hyde Park astonished and even perturbed by the things they had heard Indian or Irish nationalists saying about the British Empire.

The degree of freedom of the press existing in this country is often overrated. Technically there is great freedom, but the fact that most of the press is owned by a few people operates in much the same way as a State censorship. On the other hand freedom of speech is real. On the platform, or in certain recognised open-air spaces like Hyde Park, you can say almost anything, and, what is perhaps more significant, no one is frightened to utter his true opinions in pubs, on the tops of buses, and so forth.

The point is that the relative freedom which we enjoy depends on public opinion. The law is no protection. Governments make laws, but whether they are carried out, and how the police behave, depends on the general temper of the country. If large numbers of people are interested in freedom of speech, there will be freedom of speech, even if the law forbids it; if public opinion is sluggish, inconvenient minorities will be persecuted, even if laws exist to protect them. The decline in the desire for intellectual liberty has not been so sharp as I would have predicted six years ago, when the war was starting, but still there has been a decline. The notion that certain opinions cannot safely be allowed a hearing is growing. It is given currency by intellectuals who confuse the issue by not distinguishing between democratic opposition and open rebellion, and it is reflected in our growing indifference to tyranny and injustice abroad. And even those who declare themselves to be in favour of freedom of opinion generally drop their claim when it is their own adversaries who are being persecuted.

I am not suggesting that the arrest of five people for selling harmless newspapers is a major calamity. When you see what is happening in the world today, it hardly seems worth squealing about such a tiny incident. All the same, it is not a good symptom that such things

Freedom of speech is real.

should happen when the war is well over, and I should feel happier if this, and the long series of similar episodes that have preceded it, were capable of raising a genuine popular clamour, and not merely a mild flutter in sections of the minority press.

'The guiding principle of the State is that happiness and freedom are incompatible.'

'Freedom and Happiness'
Tribune, 4 January 1946

Several years after hearing of its existence, I have at last got my hands on a copy of Zamyatin's* *We*, which is one of the literary curiosities of this book-burning age. Looking it up in Gleb Struve's *25 Years of Soviet Russian Literature*, I find its history to have been this:

Zamyatin, who died in Paris in 1937, was a Russian novelist and critic who published a number of books both before and after the Revolution. *We* was written about 1923, and though it is not about Russia and has no direct connection with contemporary politics – it is a fantasy dealing with the twenty-sixth century A.D. – it was refused publication on the ground

---

* Publisher's note: Yevgeny Zamyatin (1884–1937).

that it was ideologically undesirable. A copy of the manuscript found its way out of the country, and the book has appeared in English, French and Czech translations, but never in Russian. The English translation was published in the United States,* and I have never been able to procure a copy: but copies of the French translation (the title is *Nous Autres*) do exist, and I have at last succeeded in borrowing one. So far as I can judge it is not a book of the first order, but it is certainly an unusual one, and it is astonishing that no English publisher has been enterprising enough to re-issue it.

The first thing anyone would notice about *We* is the fact – never pointed out, I believe – that Aldous Huxley's *Brave New World* must be partly derived from it. Both books deal with the rebellion of the primitive human spirit against a rationalised, mechanised, painless world, and both stories are supposed to take place about six hundred years hence. The atmosphere of the two books is similar, and it

---

* Publisher's note: the translation was published in 1924.

is roughly speaking the same kind of society that is being described, though Huxley's book shows less political awareness and is more influenced by recent biological and psychological theories.

In the twenty-sixth century, in Zamyatin's vision of it, the inhabitants of Utopia have so completely lost their individuality as to be known only by numbers. They live in glass houses (this was written before television was invented), which enables the political police, known as the 'Guardians,' to supervise them more easily. They all wear identical uniforms, and a human being is commonly referred to either as 'a number' or 'a unif' (uniform). They live on synthetic food, and their usual recreation is to march in fours while the anthem of the Single State is played through loudspeakers. At stated intervals they are allowed for one hour (known as 'the sex hour') to lower the curtains round their glass apartments. There is, of course, no marriage, though sex life does not appear to be completely promiscuous. For purposes of love-making everyone has a sort of ration book of pink tickets, and the partner with whom he spends one of his allotted sex hours signs the counterfoil. The Single State is ruled over by a personage known as The Benefactor, who is annually re-elected by the entire population, the vote being always unanimous. The guiding principle of the State is that happiness and freedom are incompatible. In the Garden of Eden man was happy, but in his folly he demanded freedom and was driven out into the wilderness. Now the Single State has restored his happiness by removing his freedom.

So far the resemblance with *Brave New World* is striking. But though Zamyatin's book is less well put together – it has a rather weak and episodic plot which is too complex to summarise – it has a political point which the other lacks. In Huxley's book the problem of 'human nature' is in a sense solved, because it assumes that by pre-natal treatment, drugs and hypnotic suggestion the human organism can be specialised in any way that is desired. A first-rate scientific worker is as easily produced as an Epsilon semi-moron, and in either case the vestiges of primitive instincts, such as maternal feeling or the desire for liberty, are easily dealt with. At the same time no clear reason is given why society should be stratified in the elaborate way that is described. The aim is not economic exploitation, but the desire to bully and dominate does not seem to be a motive either. There is no power-hunger, no sadism, no hardness of any kind. Those at the top have no strong motive for staying at the top, and though everyone is happy in a vacuous way, life has become so pointless that it is difficult to believe that such a society could endure.

Zamyatin's book is on the whole more relevant to our own situation. In spite of education and the vigilance of the Guardians, many of the ancient human instincts are still there. The teller of the story, D-503, who, though a gifted engineer, is a poor conventional creature, a sort of Utopian Billy Brown of London Town, is constantly horrified by the atavistic impulses which seize upon him. He falls in love (this is a crime, of course) with a certain I-330 who is a member of an underground resistance movement and succeeds for a while in leading him into rebellion. When the rebellion breaks out it appears that the enemies of The Benefactor are in fact fairly numerous, and these people, apart from plotting the overthrow of the State, even indulge, at the moment when their curtains are down, in such vices as smoking cigarettes and drinking alcohol. D-503 is ultimately saved from the consequences of his own folly. The authorities announce that they have discovered the cause of the recent disorders: it is that some human beings suffer from a disease called imagination. The nerve-centre responsible for imagination has now been located, and the disease can be cured by X-ray treatment. D-503 undergoes the operation, after which it is easy for him to do what he has known all along that he ought to do – that is, betray his confederates to the police. With complete equanimity he watches I-330 tortured by means of compressed air under a glass bell:

> She looked at me, her hands clasping the arms of the chair, until her eyes were completely shut. They took her out, brought her to

herself by means of an electric shock, and put her under the bell again. This operation was repeated three times, and not a word issued from her lips.

The others who had been brought along with her showed themselves more honest. Many of them confessed after one application. Tomorrow they will all be sent to the Machine of the Benefactor.

The Machine of the Benefactor is the guillotine. There are many executions in Zamyatin's Utopia. They take place publicly, in the presence of the Benefactor, and are accompanied by triumphal odes recited by the official poets. The guillotine, of course, is not the old crude instrument but a much improved model which literally liquidates its victim, reducing him in an instant to a puff of smoke and a pool of clear water. The execution is, in fact, a human sacrifice, and the scene describing it is given deliberately the colour of the sinister slave civilisations of the ancient world. It is this intuitive grasp of the irrational side of totalitarianism –

human sacrifice, cruelty as an end in itself, the worship of a Leader who is credited with divine attributes – that makes Zamyatin's book superior to Huxley's.

It is easy to see why the book was refused publication. The following conversation (I abridge it slightly) between D-503 and I-330 would have been quite enough to set the blue pencils working:

'Do you realise that what you are suggesting is revolution?'

'Of course, it's revolution. Why not?'

'Because there can't be a revolution. Our revolution was the last and there can never be another. Everybody knows that.'

'My dear, you're a mathematician: tell me, which is the last number?'

'What do you mean, the last number?'

'Well, then, the biggest number!'

'But that's absurd. Numbers are infinite. There can't be a last one.'

'Then why do you talk about the last revolution?'

There are other similar passages. It may well be, however, that Zamyatin did not intend the Soviet regime to be the special target of his satire. Writing at about the time of Lenin's death, he cannot have had the Stalin dictatorship in mind, and conditions in Russia in 1923 were not such that anyone would revolt against them on the ground that life was becoming too safe and comfortable. What Zamyatin seems to be aiming at is not any particular country but the implied aims of industrial civilisation. I have not read any of his other books, but I learn from Gleb Struve that he had spent several years in England and had written some blistering satires on English life. It is evident from *We* that he had a strong leaning towards primitivism. Imprisoned by the Czarist Government in 1906, and then imprisoned by the Bolsheviks in 1922 in the same corridor of the same prison, he had cause to dislike the political regime he had lived under, but his book is not simply the expression of a grievance. It is in effect a study of the Machine, the genie that man has thoughtlessly let out of its bottle and cannot put back again. This is a book to look out for when an English version appears.

**'There is no such thing as genuinely
non-political literature.'**

from 'The Prevention of Literature'
Polemic, January 1946
The Atlantic Monthly, March 1947

In England the immediate enemies of truthful-ness, and hence of freedom of thought, are the Press lords, the film magnates, and the bureau-crats, but [...] on a long view the weakening of the desire for liberty among the intellectuals themselves is the most serious symptom of all. It may seem that all this time* I have been talking about the effects of censorship, not on literature as a whole, but merely on one department of political journalism. Granted that Soviet Russia constitutes a sort of forbidden area in the British Press, granted that issues like Poland, the Span-ish civil war, the Russo-German pact, and so forth, are debarred from serious discussion, and

---

* Publisher's note: i.e. in the essay prior to this point.

that if you possess information that conflicts with the prevailing orthodoxy you are expected either to distort it or to keep quiet about it – granted all this, why should literature in the wider sense be affected? Is every writer a politician, and is every book necessarily a work of straightforward 'reportage'? Even under the tightest dictatorship, cannot the individual writer remain free inside his own mind and distil or disguise his unorthodox ideas in such a way that the authorities will be too stupid to recognise them? And if the writer himself is in agreement with the prevailing orthodoxy, why should it have a cramping effect on him? Is not literature, or any of the arts, likeliest to flourish in societies in which there are no major conflicts of opinion and no sharp distinctions between the artist and his audience? Does one have to assume that every writer is a rebel, or even that a writer as such is an exceptional person?

Whenever one attempts to defend intellectual liberty against the claims of totalitarianism, one meets with these arguments in one form or another. They are based on a complete misunderstanding of what literature is, and how – one should perhaps rather say why – it comes into being. They assume that a writer is either a mere entertainer or else a venal hack who can switch from one line of propaganda to another as easily as an organ grinder changes tunes. But after all, how is it that books ever come to be written? Above a quite low level, literature is an attempt to influence the views of one's contemporaries by recording experience. And so far as freedom of expression is concerned, there is not much difference between a mere journalist and the most 'unpolitical' imaginative writer. The journalist is unfree, and is conscious of unfreedom, when he is forced to write lies or suppress what seems to him important news: the imaginative writer is unfree when he has to falsify his subjective feelings, which from his point of view are facts. He may distort and caricature reality in order to make his meaning clearer, but he cannot misrepresent the scenery of his own mind: he cannot say with any conviction that he likes what he dislikes, or believes what he disbelieves. If he is forced to do so, the only result is that his creative faculties dry up. Nor can the imaginative writer solve the problem by keeping away from controversial topics. There is no such thing as genuinely non-political literature, and least of all in an age like our own, when fears, hatreds, and loyalties of a directly political kind are near to the surface of everyone's consciousness. Even a single tabu can have an all-round crippling effect upon the mind, because there is always the danger that any thought which is freely followed up may lead to the forbidden thought. It follows that the atmosphere of totalitarianism is deadly to any kind of prose writer, though a poet, at any rate a lyric poet, might possibly find it breathable. And in any totalitarian society that survives for more than a couple of generations, it is probable that prose literature, of the kind that has existed during the past four hundred years, must actually *come to an end*.

Literature has sometimes flourished under despotic regimes, but, as has often been pointed out, the despotisms of the past were not totalitarian. Their repressive apparatus was always inefficient, their ruling classes were usually either corrupt or apathetic or half-liberal in outlook, and the prevailing religious doctrines usually worked against perfectionism and the notion of human infallibility. Even so it is broadly true that prose literature has reached its highest levels in periods of democracy and free speculation. What is new in totalitarianism is that its doctrines are not only unchallengeable but also unstable. They have to be accepted on pain of damnation, but on the other hand they are always liable to be altered at a moment's notice. Consider, for example, the various attitudes, completely incompatible with one another, which an English Communist or 'fellow traveller' has had to adopt towards the war between Britain and Germany. For years before September 1939 he was expected to be in a continuous stew about 'the horrors of Nazism' and to twist everything he wrote into a denunciation of Hitler; after September 1939, for twenty months, he had to believe that Germany was more sinned against than sinning, and the word 'Nazi', at least so far as print went, had to drop right out of his vocabulary. Immediately after hearing the 8 o'clock news bulletin on the morning of June 22, 1941,* he had to start believing once again that Nazism was the most hideous evil the world had ever seen. Now, it is easy for a politician to make such changes: for a writer the case is somewhat different. If he is to switch his allegiance at exactly the right moment, he must either tell lies about his subjective feelings, or else suppress them altogether. In either case he has destroyed his dynamo. Not only will ideas refuse to come to him, but the very words he uses will seem to stiffen under his touch.

[...] Of course, print will continue to be used, and it is interesting to speculate what kinds of reading matter would survive in a rigidly totalitarian society. Newspapers will presumably continue until television technique reaches a higher level, but apart from newspapers it is doubtful even now whether the great mass of people in the industrialised countries feel the need for any kind of literature. They are unwilling, at any rate, to spend anywhere near as much

---

* Publisher's note: i.e. the date the Axis powers invaded the USSR, ending the Russo-German non-aggression pact.

on reading matter as they spend on several other recreations. Probably novels and stories will be completely superseded by film and radio productions. Or perhaps some kind of low-grade sensational fiction will survive, produced by a sort of conveyor-belt process that reduces human initiative to the minimum.

It would probably not be beyond human ingenuity to write books by machinery. But a sort of mechanising process can already be seen at work in the film and radio, in publicity and propaganda, and in the lower reaches of journalism. The Disney films, for instance, are produced by what is essentially a factory process, the work being done partly mechanically and partly by teams of artists who have to subordinate their individual style. Radio features are commonly written by tired hacks to whom the subject and the manner of treatment are dictated beforehand: even so, what they write is merely a kind of raw material to be chopped into shape by producers and censors. So also with the innumerable books and pamphlets commissioned by government departments. Even more machine-like is the production of short stories, serials, and poems for the very cheap magazines. Papers such as the *Writer* abound with advertisements of Literary Schools, all of them offering you readymade plots at a few shillings a time. Some, together with the plot, supply the opening and closing sentences of each chapter. Others furnish you with a sort of algebraical formula by the use of which you can construct your plots for yourself. Others offer packs of cards marked with characters and situations, which have only to be shuffled and dealt in order to produce ingenious stories automatically. It is probably in some such way that the literature of a totalitarian society would be produced, if literature were still felt to be necessary. Imagination – even consciousness, so far as possible – would be eliminated from the process of writing. Books would be planned in their broad lines by bureaucrats, and would pass through so many hands that when finished they would be no more an individual product than a Ford car at the end of the assembly line. It goes without saying that anything so produced would be rubbish; but anything that was not rubbish would endanger the structure of the state. As for the surviving literature of the past, it would have to be suppressed or at least elaborately rewritten.

Meanwhile totalitarianism has not fully triumphed anywhere. Our own society is still, broadly speaking, liberal. To exercise your right of free speech you have to fight against economic pressure and against strong sections of public opinion, but not, as yet, against a secret police force. You can say or print almost anything so long as you are willing to do it in a hole-and-corner way. But what is sinister, as I said at the beginning of this essay, is that the conscious enemies of liberty are those to whom liberty ought to mean most. The public do not care about the matter one way or the other. They are not in favour of persecuting the heretic, and they will not exert themselves to defend him. They are at once too sane and too stupid to acquire the totalitarian outlook. The direct, conscious attack on intellectual decency comes from the intellectuals themselves.

It is possible that the Russophile intelligentsia, if they had not succumbed to that particular myth, would have succumbed to another of much the same kind. But at any rate the Russian myth is there, and the corruption it causes stinks. When one sees highly educated men looking on indifferently at oppression and persecution, one wonders which to despise more, their cynicism or their short-sightedness. Many scientists, for example, are uncritical admirers of the U.S.S.R. They appear to think that the destruction of liberty is of no importance so long as their own line of work is for the moment unaffected. The U.S.S.R. is a large, rapidly developing country which has acute need of scientific workers and, consequently, treats them generously. Provided that they steer clear of dangerous subjects such as psychology, scientists are privileged persons. Writers, on the other hand, are viciously persecuted. It is true that literary prostitutes like Ilya Ehrenburg or Alexei Tolstoy are paid huge sums of money, but the only thing which is of any value to the writer as such – his freedom of expression – is taken away from him. Some, at least, of the English scientists who speak so enthusiastically of the opportunities enjoyed by scientists in Russia are capable of understanding this. But their reflection appears to be: 'Writers are persecuted in

Russia. So what? I am not a writer'. They do not see that any attack on intellectual liberty, and on the concept of objective truth, threatens in the long run every department of thought.

For the moment the totalitarian state tolerates the scientist because it needs him. Even in Nazi Germany, scientists, other than Jews, were relatively well treated, and the German scientific community, as a whole, offered no resistance to Hitler. At this stage of history, even the most autocratic ruler is forced to take account of physical reality, partly because of the lingering-on of liberal habits of thought, partly because of the need to prepare for war. So long as physical reality cannot be altogether ignored, so long as two and two have to make four when you are, for example, drawing the blueprint of an aeroplane, the scientist has his function, and can even be allowed a measure of liberty. His awakening will come later, when the totalitarian state is firmly established. Meanwhile, if he wants to safeguard the integrity of science, it is his job to develop some kind of solidarity with his literary colleagues and not regard it as a matter of indifference when writers are silenced or driven to suicide, and newspapers systematically falsified.

Any attack on intellectual liberty, and on the concept of objective truth, threatens in the long run every department of thought.

'It is not so much money and status he lacks as liberty and a world not wrecked and made soulless by the machine'

'Afterword'*

April 1946

What writers, artists, scientists and philosophers say today is indicative of future rather than current developments.

The growing power of the State produces, as we have seen, considerable dismay, particularly amongst those for whom only ten or twenty years ago Socialism was the

---

* Publisher's note: the *Manchester Evening News* published a series of four articles by Orwell in January and February 1946. Later that year they were collected and abridged for the German publication *Neue Auslese aus dem Schrifttum der Gegenwart*, under the title 'Der Aufstand der Intellektuellen' ('The Intellectual Revolt'), to which this piece was an afterword. Orwell's original English version of the afterword has not survived, and this text has been translated from the German.

guarantee of progress. But this idea has so far only gained hold of a section of the public. The magic which concepts like centralisation and planning possess today, and the idea that almost everything else can be sacrificed for economic security, still hold the masses under a spell, and their power will probably increase. It is still considered heresy to reject the materialistic version of Socialism just as thirty years ago Socialism was itself a heresy.

The antitotalitarian tendencies described are not evenly distributed among the intellectuals. Writers and artists reject the centralised State much more decisively than do scientists and engineers. We have eminent scientists who admire Soviet Russia unreservedly and even submit to the discipline of the Communist Party, while writers of both the Right and the Left do not as a rule follow the party line.

They distrust any restriction on their liberty by the State even when they are dependent on the State for economic support. On the other hand, the majority of scientists rely on the State for support of their work, which depends less on the individual and which, moreover, society regards as useful. The fact that authors like Gide, Malraux, Maritain, Koestler, and Bertrand Russell, each in his own way remains sceptical about Russian Communism and the values of the Machine Age would not of its own produce a political movement, not even if these authors were agreed among themselves. For a political movement must be not just the expression of an idea, it has also to represent the material interests of part of the population, without which no political organisation can be created. In England, where there are only two parties of any consequence, the Labour Party and the Conservative Party, attempts to found new parties have always failed because they only represented sectional interests. Even the Communist Party has never enjoyed much of a following, despite its Soviet-Russian aura, although it has at times exercised considerable influence.

One must, however, allow for the time factor. Fifty years ago a Socialist was seen here as a follower of a cause which had no chance of success, as an odd man out or a rebel, despised by the leaders of society and almost ignored by the masses. And yet today the principle of public ownership is accepted by almost everyone, including many who call themselves Conservatives. It proved acceptable because it seemed appropriate to the structure of an industrialised country and because it brought advantages for the majority of the people which unrestrained capitalism had denied them. Today the whole world is moving towards a tightly planned society in which personal liberty is being abolished and social equality unrealised. This is what the masses want, for to them security is more important than anything else. But why should this last any longer than the trend established about 1900 when private profit was the thing that mattered most? There will be a change of direction once centralisation and bureaucracy come into conflict with the interests of large groups.

Those intellectuals who today are rebels do not suffer economic hardship because almost every intellectual is better off than before. As soon as his most urgent needs are met he discovers that it is not so much money and status he lacks as liberty and a world not wrecked and made soulless by the machine: those are the things that really matter. In seeking such things, he is of course swimming against the tide. The question is, will the masses ever rebel in this way? Will the man in the street ever feel that freedom of the mind is as important and as much in need of being defended as his daily bread?

No convincing answer springs to mind, but there is one hopeful sign: the modern State, whether it wants it or not, needs constantly to raise the general level of education. Even the totalitarian State needs intelligent citizens to ensure that it is not at a disadvantage in the struggle for military and industrial supremacy.

Will the man in the street ever feel that freedom of the mind is as important and as much in need of being defended as his daily bread?

On the other hand they must be loyal and obedient and must not risk contamination by undesirable doctrines. But is it possible to educate people without at the same time exposing them to unorthodox ideas? The more educated people are – assuming that education does not just mean training in technological skills – the more they become aware of their individuality and the less will the structure of society be organised like a beehive.

Which set of ideas will gain the upper hand cannot be discussed here, but all intellectuals, whether they are opposed to centralisation and planning, or approve of a society so ordered, want to give it a more human face – whether they are believers who think genuine reform is only possible on the basis of orthodox Christian teaching or are against the whole machine of government and want only to pursue a simple, natural life – all hold one thing in common: opposition to the tyranny of the State. That so many minds in so many countries agree on this leads one to conclude that centralisation and bureaucratic controls, however much they may thrive today, will not be permitted unlimited growth.

'What is needed is the right to print what one believes to be true'

'Randall Swingler, "The Right to Free Expression" annotated by George Orwell'*

Polemic 5, September–October 1946

I have had great freedom to say what I wished, but I have only had it because I have not only ignored the pressures that are put on a writer by editors and publishers, but also public opinion inside the literary intelligentsia. Whenever I have had something that I especially wanted to

---

* Publisher's note: this text is one of eight long annotations Orwell made to an essay critical of him by Swingler (published in *Polemic* 2). Orwell's annotations were published in the margins of *Polemic* 5 alongside Swingler's original text. This specific annotation by Orwell aligned with these words in Swingler's piece: 'What in heaven is Orwell really worried about? He appears at the moment to be getting more space than any other journalist to report truthfully. Or are we to assume that he is being compelled to write lies by all the editors who offer him their columns? We are not, I am sure.'

say, I have always found that to say it at that moment was 'undesirable' and 'inopportune', and I have received the most solemn warnings against printing, sometimes from people whose opinion I respected. Mr. Swingler seems to think that it is rather profitable to be known as a hostile critic of the U.S.S.R. It may become so in the future, but during the last ten years it has been nothing of the kind, and during the past four or five years it has been extremely difficult even to get anything of anti-Russian tendency into print. My book *Animal Farm*, for instance, had to be peddled round from publisher to publisher over a period of a year or so, just as had happened earlier with my novel *Burmese Days*, which attacked another vested interest, British imperialism. Because I committed the crime known in France as *lese-Staline* I have been obliged at times to change my publisher, to stop writing for papers which represented part of my livelihood, to have my books boycotted in other papers, and to be pursued by insulting letters, articles similar to the one which Mr. Swingler has just written, and even threats of libel actions. It would be silly to complain of all this, since I have survived it, but I know that other thinner-skinned people often succumb to similar treatment, and that the average writer, especially the average young writer, is terrified of offending against the orthodoxy of the moment. For some years past, orthodoxy – at least the dominant brand of it – has consisted in not criticising Stalin, and the resulting corruption has been such that the bulk of the English literary intelligentsia has looked on at torture, massacre and aggression without expressing disapproval, and perhaps in the long run without feeling it. This may change, and in my opinion probably will change. In five years it may be as dangerous to praise Stalin as it was to attack him two years ago. But I should not regard this as an advance. Nothing is gained by teaching a parrot a new word. What is needed is the right to print what one believes to be true, without having to fear bullying or blackmail from any side.

What is needed is the right to print what one believes to be true, without having to fear bullying or blackmail from any side.

'If you carry this to its conclusion, there can be no case for allowing any political or intellectual freedom whatever.'

To George Woodcock*

4 January 1948, handwritten

Ward 3

Hairmyres Hospital

East Kilbride

Lanarkshire

Dear George,

I'd been meaning to write for some time to explain I wouldn't be coming down to London after all. As I feared, I am seriously ill, T.B. in the left lung. I've only been in the hospital about a fortnight, but before that I was in bed at home for about 2 months. I'm

---

* Publisher's note: George Woodcock was secretary of the Freedom Defence Committee, of which Orwell was vice chairman.

likely to be here for some time, because the treatment, which involves putting the lung out of action, is a slow one, & in any case I'm so pulled down & weak that I wouldn't be able to get out of bed for a couple of months or so. However, they seem confident they can patch me up all right, & I have felt a bit less like death since being here. It's a nice hospital & everyone is very kind. With luck I may be out for the summer & then I think I'll try & get a correspondent's job somewhere warm next winter. I have [had] this disease before, but not so badly, & I'm pretty sure it was the cold of last winter that started me off.

I hope the F.D.C. is doing something about these constant demands to outlaw Mosley & Co. *Tribune*'s attitude I think has been shameful, & when the other week Zilliacus wrote in demanding what amounts to Fascist legislation & creation of 2nd-class citizens, nobody seems to have replied. The whole thing is simply a thinly-disguised desire to persecute someone who can't hit back, as obviously the Mosley lot don't matter a damn & can't get a real mass following. I think it's a case for a pamphlet, & I only wish I felt well enough to write one. The central thing one has [to come] to terms with is the argument, always advanced by those advocating repressive legislation, that 'you cannot allow democracy to be used to overthrow democracy – you cannot allow freedom to those who merely use it in order to destroy freedom'. This of course is true, & both Fascists & Communists do aim at making use of democracy in order to destroy it. But if you carry this to its conclusion, there can be no case for allowing any political or intellectual freedom whatever. Evidently therefore it is a matter of distinguishing between a real & a merely theoretical threat to democracy, & no one should be persecuted for expressing his opinions, however anti-social, & no political organisation suppressed, unless it can be shown that there is a substantial threat to the stability of the state. That is the main point I should make any way. Of course there are many others.

I've done no work whatever for 2–3 months. In this place I couldn't do serious work even if I felt well, but I intend shortly to start doing an occasional book review, as I think I'm equal to that & I might as well earn some money. Richard★ was blooming when I came away, but I'm going to have him thoroughly examined, as he has of course been subjected to infection. All the best to Inge.

Yours
George

★ Publisher's note: Orwell's adopted son, born in 1944.

'Break the rules, or perish.'

'Such, Such Were the Joys'
1939?–June 1948?
(First published in *Partisan Review*, 1952)

The various codes which were presented to you at St. Cyprian's* – religious, moral, social and intellectual – contradicted one another if you worked out their implications. The essential conflict was between the tradition of nineteenth-century asceticism and the actually existing luxury and snobbery of the pre-1914 age. On the one side were low-church Bible Christianity, sex puritanism, insistence on hard work, respect for academic distinction, disapproval of self-indulgence: on the other, contempt for 'braininess' and

---

* Publisher's note: St Cyprian's was the prep school in East-bourne which Orwell attended between the ages of eight and thirteen (1911–16), before going briefly to Wellington and then to Eton as a King's Scholar.

worship of games, contempt for foreigners and the working class, an almost neurotic dread of poverty, and, above all, the assumption not only that money and privilege are the things that matter, but that it is better to inherit them than to have to work for them. Broadly, you were bidden to be at once a Christian and a social success, which is impossible. At the time I did not perceive that the various ideals which were set before us cancelled out. I merely saw that they were all, or nearly all, unattainable, so far as I was concerned, since they all depended not only on what you did but on what you *were*.

Very early, at the age of only ten or eleven, I reached the conclusion – no one told me this, but on the other hand I did not simply make it up out of my own head: somehow it was in the air I breathed – that you were no good unless you had £100,000. I had perhaps fixed on this particular sum as a result of reading Thackeray. The interest on £100,000 would be £4,000 a year (I was in favour of a safe 4 percent), and this seemed to me the minimum income that you must possess if you were to belong to the real top crust, the people in the country houses. But it was clear that I could never find my way into that paradise, to which you did not really belong unless you were born into it. You could only *make* money, if at all, by a mysterious operation called 'going into the City,' and when you came out of the City, having won your £100,000, you were fat and old. But the truly enviable thing about the topnotchers was that they were rich while young. For people like me, the ambitious middle-class, the examination passers, only a bleak, laborious kind of success was possible. You clambered upwards on a ladder of scholarships into the Home Civil Service or the Indian Civil Service, or possibly you became a barrister. And if at any point you 'slacked' or 'went off' and missed one of the rungs in the ladder, you became 'a little office boy at forty pounds a year.' But even if you climbed to the highest niche that was open to you, you could still only be an underling, a hanger-on of the people who really counted.

Even if I had not learned this from Sambo and Flip,★ I would have learned it from the other boys. Looking back, it is astonishing how intimately, intelligently snobbish we all were, how knowledgeable about names and addresses, how swift to detect small differences in accents and manners and the cut of clothes. There were some boys who seemed to drip money from their pores even in the bleak misery of the middle of a winter term. At the beginning and end of the term, especially, there was naively snobbish chatter about Switzerland, and Scotland with its ghillies and grouse moors, and 'my uncle's yacht,' and 'our place in the country,' and 'my pony' and 'my pater's touring car.' There never was, I suppose, in the history of the world a time when the sheer vulgar fatness of wealth, without any kind of aristocratic elegance to redeem it, was so obtrusive as in those years before 1914. [...] From the whole decade

---

★ Publisher's note: 'Sambo' and 'Flip' were the nicknames of the headmaster John Wilkes and his wife, both of whom illtreated and humiliated Orwell throughout his five years at the school.

before 1914 there seems to breathe forth a smell of the more vulgar, un-grown-up kinds of luxury, a smell of brilliantine and crème de menthe and soft-centre chocolates – an atmosphere, as it were, of eating everlasting strawberry ices on green lawns to the tune of the Eton Boating Song. The extraordinary thing was the way in which everyone took it for granted that this oozing, bulging wealth of the English upper and upper-middle classes would last for ever, and was part of the order of things. After 1918 it was never quite the same again. Snobbishness and expensive habits came back, certainly, but they were self-conscious and on the defensive. Before the war the worship of money was entirely unreflecting and untroubled by any pang of conscience. The goodness of money was as unmistakeable as the goodness of health or beauty, and a glittering car, a title or a horde of servants was mixed up in people's minds with the idea of actual moral virtue.

[...] By the social standards that prevailed about me, I was no good, and could not be any good. But all the different kinds of virtue seemed to be mysteriously interconnected and to belong to much the same people. It was not only money that mattered: there were also strength, beauty, charm, athleticism and something called 'guts' or 'character,' which in reality meant the power to impose your will on others. I did not possess any of these qualities. At games, for instance, I was hopeless. I was a fairly good swimmer and not altogether contemptible at cricket, but these had no prestige value, because boys only attach importance to a game if it requires strength and courage. What counted was football, at which I was a funk. I loathed the game, and since I could see no pleasure or usefulness in it, it was very difficult for me to show courage at it. Football, it seemed to me, is not really played for the pleasure of kicking a ball about, but is a species of fighting. The lovers of football are large, boisterous, nobbly boys who are good at knocking down and trampling on slightly smaller boys. That was the pattern of school life – a continuous triumph of the strong over the weak. Virtue consisted in winning: it consisted in being

bigger, stronger, handsomer, richer, more popular, more elegant, more unscrupulous than
other people – in dominating them, bullying
them, making them suffer pain, making them
look foolish, getting the better of them in every
way. Life was hierarchical and whatever happened was right. There were the strong, who
deserved to win and always did win, and there
were the weak, who deserved to lose and always
did lose, everlastingly.

I did not question the prevailing standards,
because so far as I could see there were no others. How could the rich, the strong, the elegant,
the fashionable, the powerful, be in the wrong?
It was their world, and the rules they made for
it must be the right ones. And yet from a very
early age I was aware of the impossibility of any
subjective conformity. Always at the centre of
my heart the inner self seemed to be awake,
pointing out the difference between the moral
obligation and the psychological *fact*. It was the
same in all matters, worldly or other-worldly.
Take religion, for instance. You were supposed
to love God and I did not question this. Till the

age of about fourteen I believed in God, and believed that the accounts given of him were true. But I was well aware that I did not love him. On the contrary, I hated him, just as I hated Jesus and the Hebrew patriarchs. [...] It was equally clear that one ought to love one's father, but I knew very well that I merely disliked my own father, whom I had barely seen before I was eight and who appeared to me simply as a gruff-voiced elderly man forever saying 'Don't.' It was not that one did not want to possess the right qualities or feel the correct emotions, but that one could not. The good and the possible never seemed to coincide.

There was a line of verse that I came across not actually while I was at St. Cyprian's, but a year or two later, and which seemed to strike a sort of leaden echo in my heart. It was: 'The armies of unalterable law.' I understood to perfection what it meant to be Lucifer, defeated and justly defeated, with no possibility of revenge. The schoolmasters with their canes, the millionaires with their Scottish castles, the athletes with their curly hair — these were the armies of the unalterable law. It was not easy, at that date, to realise that in fact it *was* alterable. And according to that law I was damned. I had no money, I was weak, I was ugly, I was unpopular, I had a chronic cough, I was cowardly, I smelt. This picture, I should add, was not altogether fanciful. I was an unattractive boy. St. Cyprian's soon made me so, even if I had not been so before. But a child's belief in its own shortcomings is not much influenced by facts. I believed, for example, that I 'smelt,' but this was based simply on general probability. It was notorious that disagreeable people smelt, and therefore presumably I did so too. Again, until after I had left school for good I continued to believe that I was preternaturally ugly. It was what my schoolfellows had told me, and I had no other authority to refer to. The conviction that it was *not possible* for me to be a success went deep enough to influence my actions till far into adult life. Until I was about thirty I always planned my life on the assumption not only that any major undertaking was bound to fail, but that I could only expect to live a few years longer.

176

But this sense of guilt and inevitable failure was balanced by something else: that is, the instinct to survive. Even a creature that is weak, ugly, cowardly, smelly and in no way justifiable still wants to stay alive and be happy after its own fashion. I could not invert the existing scale of values, or turn myself into a success, but I could accept my failure and make the best of it. I could resign myself to being what I was, and then endeavour to survive on those terms.

To survive, or at least to preserve any kind of independence, was essentially criminal, since it meant breaking rules which you yourself recognized. There was a boy named Cliffy Burton who for some months oppressed me horribly. He was a big, powerful, coarsely handsome boy with a very red face and curly black hair, who was forever twisting somebody's arm, wringing somebody's ear, flogging somebody with a riding crop (he was a member of Sixth Form), or performing prodigies of activity on the football field. Flip loved him (hence the fact that he was habitually called by his Christian name), and Sambo commended him as a boy who 'had character' and 'could keep order.' He was followed about by a group of toadies who nicknamed him Strong Man.

One day, when we were taking off our overcoats in the changing-room, Burton picked on me for some reason. I 'answered him back,' whereupon he gripped my wrist, twisted it round and bent my forearm back upon itself in a hideously painful way. I remember his handsome, jeering red face bearing down upon mine. He was, I think, older than I, besides being enormously stronger. As he let go of me a terrible, wicked resolve formed itself in my heart. I would get back on him by hitting him when he did not expect it. It was a strategic moment, for the master who had been 'taking' the walk would be coming back almost immediately, and then there could be no fight. I let perhaps a minute go by, walked up to Burton with the most harmless air I could assume, and then, getting the weight of my body behind it, smashed my fist into his face. He was flung backwards by the blow, and some blood ran out of his mouth. His always sanguine face turned almost black with rage. Then he turned away to rinse his mouth at the washing-basins.

'*All right!*' he said to me between his teeth as the master led us away.

For days after this he followed me about, challenging me to fight. Although terrified out of my wits, I steadily refused to fight. I said that the blow in the face had served him right, and there was an end of it. Curiously enough he did not simply fall upon me there and then, which public opinion would probably have supported him in doing. So gradually the matter tailed off, and there was no fight.

Now, I had behaved wrongly, by my own code no less than his. To hit him unawares was wrong. But to refuse afterwards to fight, knowing that if we fought he would beat me – that was far worse: it was cowardly. If I had refused because I disapproved of fighting, or because I genuinely felt the matter to be closed, it would have been all right; but I had refused merely because I was afraid. Even my revenge was made empty by that fact. I had struck the blow in a moment of mindless violence, deliberately not looking far ahead and merely determined to get my own back for once and damn the consequences. I had had time to realise that what I did was wrong, but it was the kind of crime from which you could get some satisfaction. Now all was nullified. There had been a sort of courage in the first act, but my subsequent cowardice had wiped it out.

The fact I hardly noticed was that though Burton formally challenged me to fight, he did not actually attack me. Indeed, after receiving that one blow he never oppressed me again. It was perhaps twenty years before I saw the significance of this. At the time I could not see beyond the moral dilemma that is presented to the weak in a world governed by the strong: Break the rules, or perish. I did not see that in that case the weak have the right to make a different set of rules for themselves; because, even if such an idea had occurred to me, there was no one in my environment who could have confirmed me in it. I lived in a world of boys, gregarious animals, questioning nothing, accepting the law of the stronger and avenging their own humiliations by passing them down to someone smaller. My situation was that of countless other boys, and if potentially I was more of a rebel than most, it was only because, by boyish standards, I was a poorer specimen. But I never did rebel intellectually, only emotionally. I had nothing to help me except my dumb selfishness, my inability – not, indeed, to despise myself, but to *dislike* myself – my instinct to survive.

It was about a year after I hit Cliffy Burton in the face that I left St. Cyprian's for ever. It was the end of a winter term. With a sense of coming out from darkness into sunlight I put on my Old Boy's tie as we dressed for the journey. I well remember the feeling of that brand-new silk tie round my neck, a feeling of emancipation, as though the tie had been at once a badge of manhood and an amulet against Flip's voice and Sambo's cane. I was escaping from bondage.

'Freedom is Slavery'

from *Nineteen Eighty-Four* (1949)

Winston walked over to the window, keeping his back to the telescreen. The day was still cold and clear. Somewhere far away a rocket bomb exploded with a dull, reverberating roar. About twenty or thirty of them a week were falling on London at present.

Down in the street the wind flapped the torn poster to and fro, and the word ING-SOC fitfully appeared and vanished. Ingsoc. The sacred principles of Ingsoc. Newspeak, doublethink, the mutability of the past. He felt as though he were wandering in the forests of the sea bottom, lost in a monstrous world where he himself was the monster. He was alone. The past was dead, the future was unimaginable. What certainty had he that a single human creature now living was on his side? And what way of knowing that the dominion of the Party would not endure for ever? Like an answer, the three slogans on the white face of the Ministry of Truth came back at him:

WAR IS PEACE
FREEDOM IS SLAVERY
IGNORANCE IS STRENGTH.

He took a twenty-five cent piece out of his pocket. There, too, in tiny clear lettering, the same slogans were inscribed, and on the other face of the coin the head of Big Brother. Even from the coin the eyes pursued you. On coins, on stamps, on the covers of books, on banners, on posters and on the wrapping of a cigarette packet – everywhere. Always the eyes watching you and the voice enveloping you. Asleep or awake, working or eating, indoors or out of doors, in the bath or in bed – no escape. Nothing was your own except the few cubic centimetres inside your skull. [. . .]

The telescreen struck fourteen. He must leave in ten minutes. He had to be back at work by fourteen-thirty.

Curiously, the chiming of the hour seemed to have put new heart into him. He was a lonely ghost uttering a truth that nobody would ever hear. But so long as he uttered it, in some obscure way the continuity was not broken. It was not by making yourself heard but by staying sane that you carried on the human heritage. He went back to the table, dipped his pen, and wrote:

To the future or to the past, to a time when thought is free, when men are different from one another and do not live alone – to a time when truth exists and what is done cannot be undone:

From the age of uniformity, from the age of solitude, from the age of Big Brother, from the age of doublethink – greetings!

He was already dead, he reflected. It seemed to him that it was only now, when he had begun to be able to formulate his thoughts, that he had taken the decisive step. The consequences of every act are included in the act itself. He wrote:

Thoughtcrime does not entail death: thought-crime IS death.

Now that he had recognised himself as a dead man it became important to stay alive as long as possible. Two fingers of his right hand were inkstained. It was exactly the kind of detail that might betray you. Some nosing zealot in the Ministry (a woman, probably: someone like the little sandy-haired woman or the dark-haired girl from the Fiction Department) might start wondering why he had been writing during the lunch interval, why he had used an old-fashioned pen, *what* he had been writing – and then drop a hint in the appropriate quarter. He went to the bathroom and carefully scrubbed the ink away with the gritty dark-brown soap, which rasped your skin like sandpaper and was therefore well adapted for this purpose.

He put the diary away in the drawer. It was quite useless to think of hiding it, but he could at least make sure whether or not its existence had been discovered. A hair laid across the page-ends was too obvious. With the tip of his finger he picked up an identifiable grain of whitish dust and deposited it on the corner of the cover, where it was bound to be shaken off if the book was moved.

WAR IS PEACE
FREEDOM IS SLAVERY
IGNORANCE IS STRENGTH.

'Perhaps a lunatic was simply a minority of one.'

From *Nineteen Eighty-Four* (1945)

Day and night the telescreens bruised your ears with statistics proving that people today had more food, more clothes, better houses, better recreations – that they lived longer, worked shorter hours, were bigger, healthier, stronger, happier, more intelligent, better educated, than the people of fifty years ago. Not a word of it could ever be proved or disproved. The Party claimed, for example, that today forty per cent of adult proles were literate: before the Revolution, it was said, the number had only been fifteen per cent. The Party claimed that the infant mortality rate was now only a hundred and sixty per thousand, whereas before the Revolution it had been three hundred – and so it went on. It was like a single equation with two unknowns. It might very well be that literally every word in the history books, even the things that one accepted without question, was pure fantasy. For all he knew there might never have been any such law as the *jus primae noctis*, or any such creature as a capitalist, or any such garment as a top hat.

Everything faded into mist. The past was erased, the erasure was forgotten, the lie became truth. Just once in his life he had possessed – *after* the event: that was what counted – concrete, unmistakable evidence of an act of falsification. He had held it between his fingers for as long as thirty seconds. In 1973, it must have been – at any rate, it was at about the time when he and Katharine had parted. But the really relevant date was seven or eight years earlier.

The story really began in the middle 'sixties, the period of the great purges in which the original leaders of the Revolution were wiped out once and for all. By 1970 none of them was left, except Big Brother himself. All the rest had by that time been exposed as traitors and counter-revolutionaries. Goldstein had fled and was hiding no one knew where, and of the others, a few had simply disappeared, while the majority had been executed after spectacular public trials at which they made confession of their crimes. Among the last survivors were three men named Jones, Aaronson and Rutherford. It must have been in 1965 that these three had been arrested. As often happened, they had vanished for a year or more, so that one did not know whether they were alive or dead, and then had suddenly been brought forth to incriminate themselves in the usual way. They had confessed to intelligence with the enemy (at that date, too, the enemy was Eurasia), embezzlement of public funds, the murder of various trusted Party members, intrigues against the leadership of Big Brother which had started long before the Revolution happened, and acts of sabotage causing the death of hundreds of thousands of people. After confessing to these things they had been pardoned, reinstated in the Party and given posts which were in fact sinecures but which sounded important. All three had written long, abject articles in the *Times*, analysing the reasons for their defection and promising to make amends.

Some time after their release Winston had actually seen all three of them in the Chestnut Tree Café. He remembered the sort of terrified fascination with which he had watched them out of the corner of his eye. They were men far older than himself, relics of the ancient world, almost the last great figures left over from the heroic early days of the Party. The glamour of the underground struggle and the civil war still faintly clung to them. He had the feeling, though already at that time facts and dates were growing blurry, that he had known their names years earlier than he had known that of Big Brother. But also they were outlaws, enemies, untouchables, doomed with absolute certainty to extinction within a year or two. No one who had once fallen into the hands of the Thought Police ever escaped in the end. They were corpses waiting to be sent back to the grave.

There was no one at any of the tables nearest to them. It was not wise even to be seen in the neighbourhood of such people. They were sitting in silence before glasses of the gin flavoured with cloves which was the speciality of the café. Of the three, it was Rutherford whose appearance had most impressed Winston. Rutherford had once been a famous caricaturist, whose brutal cartoons had helped to inflame popular opinion before and during the Revolution. Even now, at long intervals, his cartoons were appearing in the *Times*. They were simply an imitation of his earlier manner, and curiously lifeless and unconvincing. Always they were a rehashing of the ancient themes – slum tenements, starving children, street battles, capitalists in top hats – even on the barricades the capitalists still seemed to cling to their top hats – an endless, hopeless effort to get back into the past. He was a monstrous man, with a mane of greasy grey hair, his face pouched and seamed, with thick negroid lips. At one time he must have been immensely strong; now his great body was sagging, sloping, bulging, falling away in every direction. He seemed to be breaking up before one's eyes, like a mountain crumbling.

It was the lonely hour of fifteen. Winston could not now remember how he had come to be in the café at such a time. The place was almost empty. A tinny music was trickling from the telescreens. The three men sat in their corner almost motionless, never speaking. Uncommanded, the waiter brought fresh glasses of gin. There was a chessboard on the table beside them, with the pieces set out but no game started. And then, for perhaps half a minute in all, something happened to the telescreens. The tune that they were playing changed, and the tone of the music changed too. There came into it – but it was something hard to describe. It was a peculiar, cracked, braying, jeering note: in his mind Winston called it a yellow note. And then a voice from the telescreen was singing:

> *Under the spreading chestnut tree*
> *I sold you and you sold me:*
> *There lie they, and here lie we*
> *Under the spreading chestnut tree.*

The three men never stirred. But when Winston glanced again at Rutherford's ruinous face, he saw that his eyes were full of tears. And for the first time he noticed, with a kind of inward shudder, and yet not knowing at what he shuddered, that both Aaronson and Rutherford had broken noses.

A little later all three were re-arrested. It appeared that they had engaged in fresh conspiracies from the very moment of their release. At their second trial they confessed to all their old crimes over again, with a whole string of new ones. They were executed, and their fate was recorded in the Party histories, a warning to posterity. About five years after this, in 1973, Winston was unrolling a wad of documents which had just flopped out of the pneumatic tube onto his desk when he came on a fragment of paper which had evidently been slipped in among the others and then forgotten. The instant he had flattened it out he saw its significance. It was a half-page torn out of the *Times* of about ten years earlier – the top half of the page, so that it included the date – and it contained a photograph of the delegates at some Party function in New York. Prominent in the middle of the group were Jones, Aaronson and Rutherford. There was no mistaking them; in any case their names were in the caption at the bottom.

The point was that at both trials all three men had confessed that on that date they had been on Eurasian soil. They had flown from a secret airfield in Canada to a rendezvous somewhere in Siberia, and had conferred with members of the Eurasian General Staff, to whom they had betrayed important military secrets. The date had stuck in Winston's memory because it chanced to be midsummer day; but the whole story must be on record in countless other places as well. There was only one possible conclusion: the confessions were lies.

Of course, this was not in itself a discovery. Even at that time Winston had not imagined that the people who were wiped out in the purges had actually committed the crimes that they were accused of. But this was concrete evidence; it was a fragment of the abolished past, like a fossil bone which turns up in the wrong stratum and destroys a geological theory. It was enough to blow the Party to atoms, if in some way it could have been published to the world and its significance made known.

He had gone straight on working. As soon as he saw what the photograph was, and what it meant, he had covered it up with another sheet of paper. Luckily, when he unrolled it, it had been upside-down from the point of view of the telescreen. He took his scribbling pad on his knee and pushed back his chair, so as to get as far away from the telescreen as possible. To keep your face expressionless was not difficult, and even your breathing could be controlled, with an effort: but you could not control the beating of your heart, and the telescreen was quite delicate enough to pick it up. He let what he judged to be ten minutes go by, tormented all the while by the fear that some accident – a sudden draught blowing across his desk, for instance – would betray him. Then, without uncovering it again, he dropped the photograph into the memory hole, along with some other waste papers. Within another minute, perhaps, it would have crumbled into ashes.

That was ten – eleven years ago. Today, probably, he would have kept that photograph. It was curious that the fact of having held it in his fingers seemed to him to make a difference even now, when the photograph itself, as well as the event it recorded, was only memory. Was the Party's hold upon the past less strong, he wondered, because a piece of evidence which existed no longer *had once* existed?

But today, supposing that it could be somehow resurrected from its ashes, the photograph might not even be evidence. Already, at the time when he made his discovery, Oceania was no longer at war with Eurasia, and it must have been to the agents of Eastasia that the three dead men had betrayed their country. Since then there had been other charges – two, three, he could not remember how many. Very likely the confessions had been re-written and re-written until the original facts and dates no longer had the smallest significance. The past not only changed, but changed continuously. What most afflicted him with the sense of nightmare was that he had never clearly understood *why* the huge imposture was undertaken. The immediate advantages of falsifying the past were obvious, but the ultimate motive was mysterious. He took up his pen again and wrote:

I understand HOW: I do not understand WHY.

He wondered, as he had many times wondered before, whether he himself was a lunatic. Perhaps a lunatic was simply a minority of one. At one time it had been a sign of madness to believe that the earth goes round the sun: today, to believe that the past is unalterable. He might be *alone* in holding that belief, and if alone, then a lunatic. But the thought of being a lunatic did not greatly trouble him: the horror was that he might also be wrong.

He picked up the children's history book and looked at the portrait of Big Brother which formed its frontispiece. The hypnotic eyes gazed into his own. It was as though some huge force were pressing down upon you – something that penetrated inside your skull, battering against your brain, frightening you out of your beliefs, persuading you, almost, to deny the evidence of your senses. In the end the Party would announce that two and two made five, and you would have to believe it. It was inevitable that they should make that claim sooner or later: the logic of their position demanded it. Not merely the validity of experience, but the very existence of external reality, was tacitly denied by their philosophy. The heresy of heresies was common sense. And what was terrifying was not that they would kill you for thinking otherwise, but that they might be right. For, after all, how do we know that two and two make four? Or that the force of gravity works? Or that the past is unchangeable? If both the past and the external world exist only in the mind, and if the mind itself is controllable – what then?

But no! His courage seemed suddenly to stiffen of its own accord. The face of O'Brien, not called up by any obvious association, had floated into his mind. He knew, with more certainty than before, that O'Brien was on his side. He was writing the diary for O'Brien – to O'Brien: it was like an interminable letter which no one would ever read, but which was addressed to a particular person and took its colour from that fact.

The Party told you to reject the evidence of your eyes and ears. It was their final, most essential command. His heart sank as he thought of the enormous power arrayed against him, the ease with which any Party intellectual would overthrow him in debate, the subtle arguments which he would not be able to understand, much less answer. And yet he was in the right! They were wrong and he was right. The obvious, the silly and the true had got to be defended. Truisms are true, hold on to that! The solid world exists, its laws do not change. Stones are hard, water is wet, objects unsupported fall towards the earth's centre. With the feeling that he was speaking to O'Brien, and also that he was setting forth an important axiom, he wrote:

Freedom is the freedom to say that two plus two make four. If that is granted, all else follows.

200

**Freedom is the freedom
to say that two plus two
make four. If that is granted,
all else follows.**

Also by George Orwell

Fiction
Burmese Days
A Clergyman's Daughter
Keep the Aspidistra Flying
Coming Up for Air
Animal Farm
Nineteen Eighty-Four

Non-fiction
Down and Out in Paris and London
The Road to Wigan Pier
Homage to Catalonia
A Kind of Compulsion (1903–36)
Facing Unpleasant Facts (1937–39)
A Patriot After All (1940–41)
All Propaganda Is Lies (1941–42)
Keeping Our Little Corner Clean (1942–43)
Two Wasted Years (1943)
I Have Tried to Tell the Truth (1943–44)
I Belong to the Left (1945)
Smothered Under Journalism (1946)
It Is What I Think (1947–48)
Our Job Is to Make Life Worth Living (1949–50)
Critical Essays
Narrative Essays
Diaries
A Life in Letters
*Seeing Things As They Are: Selected Journalism
and Other Writings*

GEORGE ORWELL (1903–1950) is one of England's most famous writers and social commentators. He is the author of the classic political satire *Animal Farm* and the dystopian masterpiece *Nineteen Eighty-Four*. He is also well known for his essays and journalism, particularly his works covering his travels and his time fighting in the Spanish Civil War. His writing is celebrated for its piercing clarity, purpose and wit and his books continue to be bestsellers all over the world.